# Law for Doctors: principles and practicalities

## MA Branthwaite MD FRCP FFARCS

*Barrister, Lincoln's Inn*

*Formerly Consultant Physician and Anaesthetist*
*Royal Brompton Hospital, London, UK*

*Associate Member, Crown Office Chambers*
*One Paper Buildings, Temple, London, UK*

*Assistant Deputy Coroner*
*Inner London (South)*

PROVIDED AS
A SERVICE TO
MEDICINE BY

The ROYAL
SOCIETY of
MEDICINE
PRESS Limited

© 2000 Royal Society of Medicine Press Ltd
Reprinted 2001
1Wimpole Street, London W1G 0AE, UK
207 Westminster Road, Lake Forest, IL, 60045, USA

Apart from any fair dealing for the purposes of research or private study, criticism or review, as permitted under the UK Copyright, Designs and Patents Act, 1988, no part of this publication may be reproduced, stored, or transmitted, in any form or by any means, without the prior permission in writing of the publishers or in the case of reprographic reproduction in accordance with the terms of licences issued by the Copyright Licensing Agency in the UK, or in accordance with the terms of licences issued by the appropriate Reproduction Organisation outside the UK. Enquiries concerning reproduction outside the terms stated here should be sent to the publishers at the UK address printed on this page.

The right of Dr Margaret A Branthwaite to be identified as author of this work has been asserted by her in accordance with the Copyright, Designs and Patents Act, 1988.

**British Library Cataloguing in Publication Data**
A catalogue record for this book is available from the British Library

ISBN: 1-85315-465-2

Phototypeset by Phoenix Photosetting, Chatham, Kent

Printed in Great Britain by Bell and Bain Ltd, Glasgow

 **Preface**

Few sources of medical law are easily accessible to medical practitioners, and research is hindered by unfamiliar legal terminology and style. And yet the law is impinging on medical practice ever more frequently and creates anxiety which is exacerbated by the impotence of ignorance. 'Legal paternalism' is accepted, often gratefully, but is no more appropriate today than its medical equivalent in patient care. This book sets out to provide health care professionals, particularly doctors, with sufficient understanding of the law to alleviate as far as possible those elements of concern which are founded on uncertainty, to assist them to participate more fully in discussions and decisions on cases with which they are involved and, above all, to have some idea of what to expect, be they required to assist the court or face legal action themselves. The content is restricted to those aspects of the law which involve medical practitioners most often.

The style of a medical rather than a legal textbook has been adopted. Case reports (legal authorities) are identified numerically and collected together at the end of each chapter as references. They are also listed alphabetically in a Table of Cases at the beginning of the book, preceded by a key to the accepted abbreviations for relevant series. Wherever possible, the citation in Medical Law Reports has been chosen in preference to other legal sources. This series began in 1989 and is available at the library of the Royal Society of Medicine, as is a textbook of medical caselaw incorporating synopses of the most important actions reported before 1990. Statutes referred to in the text are listed after the Table of Cases. There is a glossary of legal terms before the index, and more detailed sources of medical law are identified at the end of chapter one. In accordance with section 6 of the Interpretation Act 1978, masculine pronouns are used throughout to indicate persons of either gender.

To the best of my knowledge and belief, the law is stated correctly as at April 1 2000.

MA Branthwaite
London, April 2000

# ▶ Contents

# ▶ Law Reports — Abbreviations

AC . . . . . . . . . . . . . . . . . . . . . . . . . . . . . . Appeal Cases
(Decisions of the House of Lords)
All ER . . . . . . . . . . . . . . . . . . . . . . . . All England Reports
BMLR . . . . . . . . . . . . . . . Butterworths Medical Law Reports
Crim LR . . . . . . . . . . . . . . . . . . . . . . Criminal Law Reports
JP . . . . . . . . . . . . . . . . . . . . . . . Justice of the Peace Reports
LJKB . . . . . . . . . . . . . . . Law Journal Reports, King's Bench
Lloyd's Rep Med . . . . . . . . . . Lloyd's Law Reports: Medical
(Continuation since 1998 of Medical Law Reports)
Med LR . . . . . . . . . . . . . . . . . . . . . . Medical Law Reports
QBD (or KB) . . . . . . . . . Queen's (or King's) Bench Division
(Queen's Bench Division of High Court)
WLR . . . . . . . . . . . . . . . . . . . . . . . . . . Weekly Law Reports

# ▶ Table of Cases

*Entries identify the chapter and the numbered reference within it.*

# ▶ Table of Statutes and Statutory Instruments

*The reference is to the page on which each Act or Instrument is mentioned*

# ▶1

# Structure and sources of English law

## Similarities between medicine and the law

Medicine and the law share a number of common characteristics. The practical applications of medicine divide broadly into medicine(physic) and surgery, the law into civil and criminal practice. Practitioners of either discipline require prolonged training, with academic (pre-clinical) studies preceding vocational (clinical) training, followed by a period of quasi-apprenticeship (pupil or house officer). Specialisation is common after full registration (call to the Bar) and practitioners may choose to adopt a continuing professional relationship with clients (GP or solicitor), or a consultative role sought only in particular circumstances (specialist or counsel).

Medicine and surgery both divide into sub-specialities and so too do civil and criminal law. Tort, or inter-personal wrong-doing short of criminality, is a sub-division of civil law which includes 'wrongs' such as negligence, nuisance, defamation and trespass to the person. Another sub-division, the law of contract, deals with disputes arising from legally enforceable agreements, although contracts for the sale of land are considered separately again. The boundaries of these legal subdivisions are not always clear cut, any more than they are in medicine.

Most litigation against medical practitioners consists of claims for the tort of negligence, although private practice also spawns claims for breach of contract. As in medicine, there is some overlap even between the primary sub-divisions – for example, gastro-intestinal haemorrhage can be managed medically or surgically. Similarly assault and battery can constitute either a criminal offence, or the civil wrong (tort) of trespass to the person. In exceptional cases, negligence is deemed so gross as to warrant prosecution as a criminal offence (see chapter 12).

The nature of legal proceedings determines the location for any hearing or trial, the status of the presiding judicial officer, and the degree of formality to be adopted in court. Such practical aspects are considered in more detail in chapters 5, 11 and12.

## Differences between medicine and the law – the role of caselaw

The similarities set out above are matched by significant differences, the most important being sources of knowledge and the way in which these are applied. Modern medicine is founded on scientific study, which may be incomplete or even erroneous, but which seeks to establish principles which can then be applied to individual cases. Case reports are no more than interesting curiosities: they are not binding truths. By contrast, English common law is built upon caselaw – the body of decided judgments in individual cases which together form legal principles. These principles are then applied in subsequent cases unless the new matter can be distinguished on its facts from all the preceding decisions, or new and cogent argument for change can be advanced. A single case report, sometimes of consider-able antiquity, can suffice to secure a contested point unless that decision has been specifically over-ruled by a more recent and authoritative judgment.

## Legal precedent

This term describes the binding power of previous decisions on the deter-mination of subsequent, similar cases. It is intended to secure parity of treatment. Decisions in the High Court are binding upon lower courts such as those presided over by Magistrates and Coroners, and are usually, but not necessarily, followed in subsequent High Court judgments. Decisions by the Appellate Courts (Court of Appeal and House of Lords) are binding on all lower courts and, although the House of Lords has a power to reverse a decision of its own, this is only invoked very rarely.

## Statutory law

Superimposed upon common law – the legacy of decided cases – are the provisions of statute. Statutes are Acts of Parliament brought into force on a designated date after completion of a series of procedural steps, culminat-ing in the grant of Royal assent. Such parliamentary legislation may define an issue not previously subject to exploration in the courts, or it may consolidate principles established at common law into a legally-binding statute. Many Acts create a power to delegate subsidiary decision-making to a designated Minister, local authority or other official. This 'subordinate legislation' can be actioned swiftly and simply when need arises, to make changes to detail as distinct from principle. If there are concerns that the power has been used improperly, application can be made by properly interested persons for judicial review. This means that ministerial decisions are subject to review by the courts – ie the judiciary. This contrasts with Acts of Parliament which can only be rescinded or amended by further legislation. There is no power for an English parliament to limit the discretion of its successors.

## European Law

The United Kingdom joined the European Community in 1973. The enabling legislation (European Communities Act 1972) required that all provisions of Community law intended to take direct effect in the UK shall do so, whether made before or after the Act came into force. This meant that despite the centuries-old tradition of the absolute sovereignty of Parliament, UK Acts were, from then on, subject to Community law. When called upon to interpret statutory law, the domestic courts must do so in conformity with EC law. Matters of conflict are referred to the European Court of Justice, usually after a series of domestic appeals ultimately reaching the House of Lords. Once the European Court has given its decision on the specific point of law, the case is returned to the English courts for final determination in the light of the European ruling.

The Human Rights Act 1998 incorporates into English law the European Convention for the Protection of Human Rights and Fundamental Freedoms and comes into force in October 2000. The UK was an original signatory to the Convention in 1950, but did not incorporate its terms into domestic law. In future, claimants seeking to assert a right under the Convention will be able to do so in the English courts instead of applying to the European Court of Human Rights. There are predictions that the volume of domestic litigation will increase significantly as a result.

## The law in Scotland and Northern Ireland

English common law applies in England and Wales. It is similar in principle in Northern Ireland but there are some differences too, for example, proceedings in the coroners court. The law in Scotland is different in both structure and principle and has more in common with the continental system known, confusingly, as civil law. Fortunately the differences of principle between English and Scots law relating to clinical negligence are minor and are not considered here.

## Legislative basis for the regulation of health care

A series of statutes defines the components and organisation of the NHS. The most important current statutes are the National Health Service Act 1977, the NHS and Community Care Act 1990, the NHS Primary Care Act of 1997 and the Health Act 1999. Regulations governing the availability and prescribing of medicinal products are also enshrined in statute and so too are the powers to register and regulate the performance of medical practitioners. A number of other statutes apply to specific aspects of medical practice, eg assisted reproduction, transplantation.

## Sources of legal authority

Compendia of statutes and statutory instruments are published and updated regularly. Legislation introduced recently is also available without restriction on the internet. Caselaw is available in published series, some of which are available electronically in whole or in part, but only to subscribers. Recent judgments of the High Court and Appellate courts are posted on the internet.

Law reports – referred to as 'authorities' – are published both in official series, identified according to the court in which the hearing was held, and unofficial series which are more eclectic. Accepted abbreviations are used to identify the series; those used here are explained in front of the Table of Cases. The year of publication is often an essential identifying feature and, if so, is entered in square brackets []. If the date is no more than an ancillary to identification, for example where there are consecutive journal numbers, the year is quoted in round brackets (). The date precedes the abbreviation for the series, followed by the page number, often with a subsidiary reference to a particular passage in the judgment. Many series include a head-note or summary. These are not part of the official judgment and should be used cautiously. There are also 'casebooks' containing abstracts of reports on specific legal topics, often accompanied by useful and authoritative comment. A small number of long-established textbooks, usually referred to by the name of the original author, also have status as legal authority and may be quoted in court. The national press, particularly

*The Times* Law Reports, includes some detailed and authoritative reports which are accepted as legal authority if the case is not reported elsewhere.

*Reports of medical caselaw* have been available as a single series since 1989, first published by BMP (Business and Medical Publications) then without change of title by Oxford University Press and, since 1998, with a new title and format as one of the Lloyd's law report series. A less widely consulted series is Butterworth's Medical Law Reports. Cases before the late 1980's must be sought in non-specialist series. Inquests are not reported formally but appeals arising from them appear in Justice of the Peace Reports and sometimes in the independent series as well.

## Access to Sources of Legal Authority

Statutes and Statutory Instruments from 1996:    www.hmso.gov.uk/acts.htm
and www.hmso.gov.uk/stat.htm
Recent decisions of the House of Lords:
www.parliament.the-stationery-office.co.uk
Court of Appeal and High Court decisions:
http://wood.ccta.gov.uk/courtser/judgements.nsf

Other useful sites include:

| | |
|---|---|
| www.lawalert.net | Headnotes of new commercial and common law decisions |
| www.venables.co.uk | Up to date information on access to legal information |
| www.smithbernal.com | Global court reporting and litigation support group |
| www.courtservice.gov.uk | Access to recent decisions, including coroners' law |
| www.context.co.uk/preview.html | Caselaw on compact disc |
| postmaster@iclr.co.uk | Incorporated Council of Law Reporting (England & Wales) |
| www.lawreports.co.uk | Daily Law Notes. |

*Textbooks on medical law* include

| | |
|---|---|
| Jones MA. | Medical Negligence, 2nd Edition. Sweet & Maxwell 1996 |
| Kennedy I & Grubb A.(Eds) | Principles of Medical Law. Oxford University Press 1998. An annual update is published as a cumulative supplement. |

Matthews P & Foreman J.    Jervis on the Office and Duties of Coroners, 11th Edition.
Sweet & Maxwell, 1993. Regular supplements also available.

Powers MJ & Harris N (Eds)    Clinical Negligence, 3rd Edition. Butterworths, 2000.

*Casebooks on medical law* include

Kennedy I & Grubb A.    Medical Law: text and materials 2nd Edition. Butterworths, 1994.

Knapman P & Powers MJ.    Sources of Coroners' Law. Barry Rose, 1999.

Nelson-Jones R & Burton F.    Medical Negligence Caselaw. 1st Ed Fourmat Publishing, 1990.
2nd Ed Butterworths, 1995.

Stauch M, Wheat K.    Sourcebook on Medical Law. Cavendish Publishing, 1998.

# ►2

# Principles of negligence; duty and standard of care

## Legal basis for claims arising from clinical practice

Clinical negligence, a term used in preference to medical negligence to encompass actions against all health professionals, is a sub-section of the law of tort, a generic term for civil wrong-doing. The legal criteria for a finding of negligence are

► the existence of a duty of care owed by one person to another

► breach of the duty of care

► foreseeable injury occurring as a consequence of the breach.
All three elements of the test must be fulfilled if the claimant is to succeed[1].

Private medical practice generates claims founded on breach of contract as well as negligence. A contract is an agreement creating obligations recognised and enforceable by law. It requires

► offer

► acceptance

► consideration – 'the price for which the promise is bought'.

No consideration passes directly between NHS patient and the practitioner or treating hospital. There is no legally enforceable, individual contract. Claims alleging wrongful medical practice within an NHS hospital are therefore virtually always brought in tort. By contrast, claims arising in private practice are often brought in both contract and tort. However, the allegations of wrong-doing (misfeasance) cited as the elements of the tort or contractual default are often identical.

## Parties to the action

Surviving adult patients of sound mind who seek redress for perceived clinical error take legal action in their own name. Actions on behalf of children (below 18 years) and those without the necessary mental capacity are brought in their name by a nominated and court-approved 'litigation friend'. Actions arising from the death of a patient are brought by the executor or administrator and often encompass a claim for damages on behalf of the estate of the deceased as well as a claim for financial support for the deceased's dependants.

Actions in negligence lie against the person or persons who owed the duty of care. Institutions such as hospitals can be identified as 'persons' for legal purposes and, since 1990, NHS hospitals have carried vicarious liability for medical as well as other employed staff. It is therefore now usual for the Trust to be cited as the defendant whereas actions against general practitioners still lie against the individual. Similarly, private practitioners are either pursued individually or are identified as a co-defendant with a private hospital. Claims brought against more than one defendant raise conflict between them and occasionally a defendant may seek to transfer responsibility for an adverse outcome to a third party (now called a 'part 20 claim'). These conflicts complicate the legal process but do not undermine the application of legal principle.

Other factors which affect conduct of an action are the value and complexity of the claim and how the parties are funded. Chapters 5 and 7 respectively cover the current legal process and funding.

## Duty of care

The professional obligation of doctors to their patients suffices to found a common law duty of care, reinforced within the National Health Service by the provisions of health service legislation. Sometimes however a doctor's primary duty is to some other individual or organisation, for example, medical examinations for the purposes of employment or insurance[2]. Here the doctor-patient relationship does not exist in conventional terms but the practitioner still has a duty to avoid causing harm. Occasional differences exist between professional and legal obligations, for example, if a child dies during the course of medical treatment, there is a *professional* duty to explain to parents the reasons for and circumstances of the death[3]. However the giving of such information does not create a *legal* duty of care because it does not found a doctor-patient relationship and there is no free-standing duty of candour[4].

## Standard of care

At English law the standard required of medical practitioners is determined by judicial analysis of professional opinion. A doctor is not to be deemed negligent if acting in accordance with the opinion of a responsible body of medical practitioners, skilled and practised in that art[5]. This traditional 'Bolam' test, so named from the case in which the principle was first enunciated, has been refined more recently by a requirement that medical opinion on which the court is invited to rely must also be 'reasonable', in other words it must be formulated on the basis of a considered evaluation of the risks and benefits associated with a particular procedure and thus be capable of withstanding logical analysis[6]. When expert opinion conflicts, the Judge is not permitted merely to prefer one opinion to another but must decide between them by assessing their rationality. However, the court will be slow to reject the sincerely held views of distinguished experts, and due consideration is also given to the different standards which may apply to sub-specialities[7], even though numerically small. Finally and very importantly, the standard to be determined is that which applied at the time of the events in question, *not* at the time of trial[8].

In some instances, guidelines or protocols are cited as a means of defining proper standards, a trend which can be expected to escalate as the National Institute for Clinical Excellence makes recommendations. Important though such guidelines are, legally as well as in practice, they are better considered as indicative of an accepted course of practice rather than the final arbiter of professional standards. Any alternative would stifle the progress of medicine. However, if legal action is brought because harm results from transgression of guidelines or protocols *without good reason*, the claimant is very likely to succeed.

# The role of the hospital

The Health Act 1999 imposes a *statutory* duty on Health Authorities, Primary Care Trusts and NHS Trusts to monitor and improve the quality of health care, and establishes the Commission for Health Improvement to inform, advise and review this function. Until this legislative intervention, the basis for imposing liability on a hospital rested on the common law (decided cases), and the principle that an employing authority is vicariously responsible for the negligent actions of its staff[9,10]. The primary duty is to patients. The personal welfare of staff is included[11], but the duty does not extend to unidentified third parties harmed by the patient of a hospital[12].

Although the court may sympathise with a junior doctor called upon to undertake tasks beyond his competence, the legal position is that hospitals should have in place systems and staff with sufficient experience and expertise to ensure an appropriate standard of care is provided to all patients[13-15]. This must be right from the perspective of the patient but raises obvious difficulties when financial or human resources are restricted. Claims based upon failure to provide a service at all because of insufficient funding are less likely to succeed and, in general, the courts are reluctant to interfere with decisions, taken in good faith, on the allocation of scarce resources[16]. However, 'blanket bans' on a particular procedure have been challenged successfully[17], as has a decision to close a specialist unit, albeit with criticism directed to the procedure rather than the principle[18]. Actions of this nature seek a remedy for alleged maladministration, not compensation for negligently-inflicted personal injury. The appropriate legal process is therefore not an action in tort but *Judicial Review* – a procedure available, with leave, in carefully defined circumstances and to 'properly interested persons'. It remains to be seen whether the Human Rights Act 1998, which comes into force on October 2 2000, will prompt claims based upon contravention of Article 2 of the European Convention on Human Rights – the right to life. It is at least arguable that Health Authorities will be obliged to provide medical care in all cases where life might otherwise be endangered and that lack of resources will not be accepted as a valid defence.

# References

1. Barnett v Chelsea & Kensington HMC [1969] 1QB 428; 2 WLR 422.
   Casualty officer declined to attend three nightwatchmen who were vomiting after drinking tea; one died later from arsenical poisoning. Claim failed. Breach of duty established but no causation – man would have died anyway.
2. R v Croydon HA [1998] Lloyd's Rep Med 44
   Failure to diagnosis pulmonary hypertension on a pre-employment chest X-ray. Breach of duty admitted but obligations assumed by the radiologist did not extend to claimant's private life (decision to have a child). See also *Kapfunde v Abbey National & Dr D Daniel [1999] 2 Lloyd's Rep Med 48*. Occupational health report adverse to claimant's application for employment. No duty of care by practitioner; no vicarious laibility by employer.
3. General Medical Council: Good Medical Practice 1998 para 17.
   Paragraphs 16 – 21 cover 'when things go wrong' and deal with general duty of disclosure.
4. Powell & Another v Boladz *et al* [1998] Lloyd's Rep Med 116.
   Doctor-patient relationship not established if practitioner treating a patient who has died informs relatives what happened. Parents of deceased child had no cause of action for psychiatric injury attributed to alleged cover-up.
5. Bolam v Friern Hospital Management Committee [1957] 1 WLR 583.
   Claimant suffered fractures during ECT administered without muscle relaxants, a technique endorsed at the time by a 'responsible body of medical opinion'. Test for breach of duty set out by McNair J in directions to jury.
6. Bolitho v City & Hackney HA [1998] Lloyd's Rep Med 26.
   Negligent failure to attend a child's respiratory crisis. Court is not necessarily bound by expert opinion. Support by distinguished experts will usually demonstrate reasonableness of an opinion but if, in rare cases, expert opinion is incapable of withstanding logical analysis, judge is entitled to find it is not reasonable or responsible.

7. **Defrietas v O'Brien & Another [1993] 4 Med LR 281.**
   Exploratory spinal surgery in absence of clear clinical or radiological indications to operate. Spinal surgeons deemed to form a category of specialism separate and apart from other orthopaedic and neurosurgeons.

8. **Roe v Ministry of Health [1954] 2 WLR 915.**
   Paraplegia following spinal anaesthesia; ampoules stored in phenol which leached through invisible cracks in the glass. The claim failed: must not look at 1947 accident with 1954 spectacles. (Cause identified & reported in 1951).

9. **Cassidy v Ministry of Health [1951] 1 All ER 574.**
   Surgery and splinting for Dupuytren's contracture; severe post-operative pain; flexion deformity of four fingers. Hospital responsible for adverse outcome, however caused, through its duty to appoint responsible staff.

10. **M v Calderdale and Kirklees HA [1998] Lloyds Rep Med 157.**
    Termination of pregnancy, contracted to a private hospital by Health Authority, was undertaken negligently and failed. Health Authority responsible – had a non-delegable duty to ensure appropriate standards were offered.

11. **Ogden v Airedale HA [1996] 7 Med LR 153**
    Faulty working conditions permitted Radiographer to become sensitised to X-ray chemicals, developing asthma. Awarded damages for his condition, loss of earnings, loss of chosen career and loss of job security.

12. **Palmer v Tees HA, Hartlepool & East Durham NHS Trust [1999] Lloyds Rep Med 351.**
    Psychotic patient murdered a child and mutilated her body a year after hospital discharge. Alleged to have told staff of sexual feelings towards children and that a child would be murdered. Claim on behalf of child and mother struck out – insufficient proximity between hospital and unknown victim to found a duty of care.

13. **Wilsher v Essex AHA [1988] AC 1074.**
    Failure by junior doctor in special care baby unit to recognise misplaced umbilical artery catheter. Health Authority *may be* directly liable to patient for failing to provide sufficient qualified and competent medical staff.

14. **Bull v Devon AHA [1993] 4 Med LR 117.**
    Birth asphyxia in second twin. Health Authority liable for failure to provide and implement efficient system for alerting appropriate staff on call to an impending emergency.

15. **Robertson v Nottingham HA [1997] 8 Med LR 1.**
    Brain damaged infant – foetal distress before onset of labour. Health Authority had a non-delegable duty to establish proper systems of care and can be liable for a 'systems failure'.

16. **R v Cambridge HA ex parte B (A Minor) [1995] 6 Med LR 250.**
    Decision not to provide unproven treatment for relapse of leukaemia in a child. Court is not the arbiter of merit. Health Authority is legally charged with making decision and is not to be required to present accounts.

17. **R v NW Lancs HA ex parte A, D & G. *The Times*, August 24 1999.**
    Policy not to fund gender reassignment surgery extra-contractually, other than in very exceptional cases, was 'almost a blanket ban'. Rationing accepted as inevitable but must be based on proper assessment of competing need.

18. **R v NW Thames RHA *et al ex parte* Daniels [1993] 4 Med LR 364.**
    Health Authority erred in failing to consult interested parties before closing a bone marrow transplant unit *but* no public law remedy was granted because none would have benefited the applicant.

# ▶3
# Foreseeability and causation

The third limb of the test for negligence is itself tripartite. The claimant must establish that

▶ foreseeable

▶ injury

▶ occurred as a result of the breach of the duty of care.

## Foreseeability

Complications arising in the course of medical treatment are sometimes wholly unexpected. In legal terms however, an injury is deemed to be a foreseeable consequence of the negligent act if *damage of that general nature* can be foreseen. Thus although anterior spinal artery syndrome would not be cited as a specific risk of induced hypotension during anaesthesia, injury caused by under-perfusion of major organs – including nervous tissue – *is* a foreseeable consequence[1]. Such a complication was therefore deemed to lie within the risk created by a technique of hypotensive anaesthesia considered negligent, despite publication of a large series in a peer-reviewed journal.

## Injury

Actions in negligence are brought to secure compensation for harm suffered as a result of the wrongful act. Without an injury causally related to the tort, there is no basis for a claim. This contrasts with actions in battery where the mere fact of unlawful (ie non-consensual) touching warrants compensation, whether or not injury has occurred as a consequence.

Injury which founds a claim for damages can be physical, mental or economic. However, the courts are more willing to compensate physical rather than either mental or economic injury. The victim of a negligent act who suffers psychiatric injury in circumstances where personal injury of some kind is reasonably foreseeable is deemed a 'primary victim' and is entitled to compensation. Conversely, a claimant who suffers psychiatric injury from witnessing the consequences of negligence is a 'secondary victim' and can only recover if able to show a close emotional bond with the victim, proximity in time and place to the accident or its immediate aftermath, and reasonable foreseeability that an onlooker of normal fortitude would suffer mental distress resulting in psychiatric illness[2]. Economic loss which is consequent upon negligently inflicted physical or mental injury, for example, loss of earnings or costs of care, is recoverable. However the courts are reluctant to award damages for pure economic loss. In a recent decision[3], the House of Lords rejected the previously accepted view that the costs of bringing up a child conceived as a result of a negligent sterilisation can be recovered as part of a 'personal injury'.

## Causation of injury

An adverse outcome from medical treatment, even when unexpected, does not suffice to establish a finding of clinical negligence. There must be a causal link with breach of duty. This means it is necessary to establish that the adverse outcome would not have occurred as a result of the natural progression of disease, and was not a foreseeable and accepted complication of treatment carried out to the highest possible standard. Once again the courts rely upon expert medical opinion but, when considering causation rather than breach of duty, evidence from the most recent sources can be adduced. Sometimes a negligent act is no more than a contributory factor in determining an adverse outcome. Then the court will endeavour to identify and award compensation proportional to that element of the injury. However, if the negligently-caused element of the injury cannot be distinguished, the claimant can succeed in full provided the negligence made a 'material contribution' – in other words was more than de minimis[4].

## Injury caused by failure to act

Here the court is faced with a hypothetical situation: what would have been the outcome had there not been a negligent failure to act? In some cases this requires evaluation of the natural progression of untreated disease and, after hearing expert evidence, the judge will make a finding of 'fact' – legal fact – as to what would have occurred but for the negligence. If the adverse outcome is deemed to have been determined before the negligent act, or to have been more likely than not in any event, then the claim fails outright – there is no recovery for the lost chance[5]. However, if there was a greater than 50% chance of a good outcome but for the negligent failure to act, the claimant succeeds and damages are calculated according to the magnitude of the lost chance[6]. There is currently a move towards accepting that loss of less than even a 50% chance should found a successful claim in tort, in proportion to the magnitude of the lost opportunity.

A further difficulty is created if the negligent failure to act does not have agreed consequences. Thus if a practitioner fails to attend a patient, the court must determine what *that individual practitioner* would have done if properly attending, and thereafter consider what the practitioner *should* have done if acting in accordance with a responsible body of medical opinion[7,8]. The first question is one of fact. The second requires judicial assessment of professional opinion.

## The burden and standard of proof

It is incumbent on the claimant to establish his case[9]. First the facts must be established and thereafter the successful claimant must satisfy the judge on all three elements of negligence – existence of a duty, breach of duty, and foreseeable injury occurring as a result. The facts may be a matter of contention between the parties, particularly if contemporaneous notes are inadequate, missing, or contain obvious alterations suggesting late amendment. If there is conflict and the matter reaches court, the judge is responsible for making a determination of 'fact' in the light of the evidence presented and his view of the credibility of the witnesses. On causation of injury, the claimant need only establish to the satisfaction of the judge that the adverse outcome was causally related to the alleged negligence *on the balance of probabilities*. This is a far less stringent test than *beyond reasonable doubt* which is the standard required by criminal law.

## *Res ipsa loquitur*

'The thing speaks for itself'. This aphorism is merely a means of drawing an inference of negligence and seeks to imply the adverse outcome is such that no other explanation is tenable. It is sometimes pleaded on behalf of a claimant who cannot know what, in fact, transpired – such as cardiac arrest occurring during general anaesthesia. The defendant must then adduce evidence to rebut the presumption of negligence by offering a plausible, non-negligent explanation. There is no obligation on the defendant to prove the non-negligent explanation was the more likely cause of the catastrophe. It may also be possible to refute the inference of negligence by satisfying the judge that proper care *was* exercised and that the adverse outcome was either extremely rare or impossible to explain in the light of current knowledge[10].

## The incomplete case

The requirement to prove a causal link between adverse outcome and breach of duty often presents an insuperable hurdle to the claimant bringing action in clinical negligence. This can be so even when breach of duty has been admitted by the defendant. Many patients have difficulty understanding why their claim has failed when breach of duty is clear, obvious or even admitted. However the legal process is 'all or none' and there is no legally enforceable remedy for breach of duty unless consequential injury can also be established. Alternative dispute resolution may permit exploration of alternatives to an award of damages and is considered in chapter 6.

## References

1. Hepworth v Kerr [1995] 6 Med LR 139.
   Anterior spinal artery thrombosis attributed to excessive and unduly prolonged induced hypotension during general anaesthesia. Injury was but a variant of the foreseeable and within the risk created by the negligence.
2. Page v Smith [1996] AC 155.
   House of Lords decision restricting the circumstances in which an onlooker ('secondary victim') can secure compensation for psychiatric injury caused by witnessing distressing events.
3. McFarlane v Tayside Health Board [2000] Lloyd's Rep Med 1.
   Pain and inconvenience of child-bearing arising from negligent failure of sterilisation is to be compensated but the costs of rearing the child are not recoverable. House of Lords decision reversing earlier caselaw.
4. Bonnington Castings Ltd v Wardlaw [1956] AC 613.
   Silicosis attributable to *both* negligent and non-negligent exposure to dust. Negligence made a material contribution and, although unable to demonstrate there would have been no injury but for the negligence, claimant succeeded.
5. Hotson v East Berks AHA [1987] AC 750.
   Delayed diagnosis of slipped epiphysis. Award of damages in proportion to magnitude of lost chance of a good outcome was reversed on appeal because an adverse outcome was already more likely than not.
6. Judge v Huntingdon HA [1995] 6 Med LR.
   Negligent delay in diagnosis of breast cancer resulted in loss of an 80% chance of cure. *Quantification of the loss* was calculated on this basis. This contrasts with the 'all or nothing' approach to causation (see 5).

7. Joyce v Merton, Sutton & Wandsworth HA [1996] 7 Med LR 1.

Allegedly negligent failure to consult a vascular surgeon when a weak pulse and cool limb followed brachial arteriotomy. The *Bolam* test is to be applied to determine what constitutes proper care.

8. Bolitho v City & Hackney HA [1998] AC 232 and [1998] Lloyd's Rep Med 26.

House of Lords confirmed tests to be applied to determine consequence of a failure to act: what *would* the practitioner have done and what *should* the practitioner have done.

9. Wilsher v Essex AHA [1988] AC 1074.

Retinopathy of prematurity occurred after negligent exposure to high concentrations of oxygen. Plaintiff failed to establish that oxygen toxicity, as distinct from other possible causes, was responsible in part or at all.

10. Ratcliff v Plymouth & Torbay HA *et al* [1998] Lloyd's Rep Med 162.

Unexplained neurological defect after spinal anaesthesia. Court satisfied on balance of probabilities that proper care had been exercised, even though no satisfactory explanation for injury was offered. Plea of *res ipsa loquitur* failed.

# ▶4
# Financial compensation

The outcome of a successful claim in negligence is an award of damages, a payment made to compensate the claimant for the injury caused by the negligence and for its consequences. The intention is to restore the claimant, so far as money is able, to the position he would have been in but for the negligent act. Damages are not intended to be punitive or to exact retribution, and the size of the award bears no relationship to the perceived or actual magnitude of the alleged wrongdoing. Very occasionally an award is enhanced to compensate the claimant for additional injury caused to feelings or pride by the defendant's unacceptable behaviour, but identifying a separate, punitive component – 'aggravated damages' – has been deemed inappropriate in clinical actions because it conflicts with the general principle of compensation[1]. This contrasts with the United States where an award of damages can include a punitive element as well as compensation.

## General damages

This is the sum awarded for pain, suffering and loss of amenity attributable to the injury. The impact of the same injury, for example a facial scar, may differ between individuals because of inherent personal characteristics such as sex, age, activities or special hobbies. Some account is taken of such differences in determining the magnitude of general damages but overall there should be reasonable parity between awards for like injuries. Figures are based upon Judicial Studies Board Guidelines which are determined and updated regularly and which set a range within which awards for a particular injury are usually selected. Caselaw is used in argument to establish or refute a particular point within any guideline range. In a report published in December 1999, the Law Commission recommended that general damages in England and Wales were too low by comparison with other jurisdictions and should be increased by between 50 and 100%. Test cases seeking to effect this recommendation were heard in March 2000 by the Court of Appeal. Some increase in general damages was deemed appropriate but by not more than one third, with no increase for claims valued at less than £10,000[2].

*Interest* is awarded on general damages at 2% from the date on which proceedings were served to the date of trial. The low rate reflects the valuation of damages as at the date of trial.

## Special damages

This term covers all losses, attributable to the negligently caused injury, which are specific to the individual. Past losses such as interruption of earnings, care and travel costs are amenable to reasonably accurate calculation whereas future losses are hypothetical. However even past losses are difficult to determine if there has been long delay between the injury and the conclusion of trial, or detailed records have not been kept – for example by an individual who is self-employed.

*Interest* on past losses is recoverable from the date of injury to the date of trial and is awarded at half the 'appropriate rate'. The appropriate rate is the average allowed on the High Court Special Investment Account over the relevant period. Half the appropriate rate is chosen to reflect the fact that some of the past losses will have occurred soon after the injury whereas others are still on-going at the time of trial. The only exception is interest on the statutory bereavement award and funeral expenses, which are recoverable after a fatal accident. Interest on these two elements is at the full appropriate rate from date of death to date of trial.

## The concept of multiplier and multiplicand

Serious injury can have repercussions for an individual and his family which persist throughout and beyond his lifetime. The court seeks to determine the totality of the loss at the time of trial or settlement and this entire sum is then available, either directly to the adult claimant of sound mind, or within the safe-keeping of the court for the benefit of minors and those of unsound mind. This 'accelerated receipt' means the claimant has the immediate benefit of funds which, but for the injury, would have taken a lifetime to acquire (earn) or to require (care costs). If these funds are invested wisely, additional income is generated and the capital increases in value to keep pace with inflation. An allowance must therefore be made to offset this effect when calculating the sum to be awarded in damages. Unpredictable variables and uncertainties for the individual must also be acknowledged in calculating now what losses or needs may ensue in the future.

The *multiplicand* is the annual net value of each element of future loss or expense, based upon figures which are current at the date of trial.

The *multiplier* is the number of years over which the loss or expense is expected to occur, offset to allow for accelerated receipt and the uncertainties of predicting an individual's future.

Tables of multipliers have been constructed according to the rate of return anticipated on investments. Traditionally a figure of 4.5% was chosen but, in a landmark decision by the House of Lords[3], the greater security of index-linked government stock was deemed appropriate and henceforth multipliers were to be selected on the basis of a 3% return. Currently there is a pressure to select multipliers on a 2% basis. The financial consequences are enormous. For example, the multiplier for a male claimant aged 20 at the time of trial and with a normal life expectancy (say 55 years) increases from 20.62 if the rate of return on investments is 4.5%, to 27.4 at 3% and 34.3 at 2%. In the context of actions arising within the National Health Service, there is an obvious conflict between the need properly to compensate an individual harmed by negligently delivered medical treatment and the requirement to ensure limited resources are available to provide high quality care to the public at large. On the broader scene, the conflict lies between adequate compensation for the individual and the cost of insurance for the majority.

## Provisional damages

The consequences of injury are not always apparent immediately. Some allowance for future deterioration may be made by the award of a percentage of the additional damages which would be appropriate were the adverse event to ensue, selected according to the likelihood of this happening. Alternatively there is a legal mechanism which permits an award of provisional damages at trial *provided* there is a real (ie admitted or proven) chance that at some future date the claimant will, as a result of the negligent act, develop some serious disease or suffer some serious deterioration in his physical or mental condition. This means the claimant is compensated at the time of trial only for the existing injury but has the right, for a specified number of years, to claim further recompense if the adverse future development does indeed occur.

## Some specific elements of loss

Some heads of claim are easy to identify such as loss of earnings, pension rights or a requirement for new or adapted housing to accommodate the needs of a disabled person. High earning claimants secure far higher awards than those with low or no income because, without the negligent injury, they and their families would have enjoyed the benefits of the higher income. The purpose of the award is to compensate them for their loss. The apparent injustice of 'to he that hath shall more be given' is illusory because the award is not based on some generally applicable notional income but on the previous situation and potential of the individual.

If there is no measurable and predictable earnings loss, a claim may be allowed for compromise on the labour market, often known as a *Smith & Manchester* award. This may also be appropriate for a young child whose career options are indeterminate at the time of trial. Alternatively the future losses of children are calculated according to national average earnings in careers comparable to those of their parents or siblings. Such awards are never high because there is a large element of accelerated receipt and the loss is of a chance, not of a defined achievement. If an attempt is made to calculate an actual future loss on the basis of an intended career, the award is likely to be discounted for the perceived magnitude of the chance that the claimant's intention would be fulfilled.

*Fatal accidents* give rise to claims on behalf of the estate of the deceased (Law Reform (Miscellaneous Provisions) Act 1934) and those dependent on the deceased at the time of death (Fatal Accidents Act 1976). The calculation of special damages is particularly difficult because losses before trial, as well as those in the future, are hypothetical. In addition to any proven individual losses, close relatives (spouses and parents of children less than 18 years) are entitled to a statutory bereavement award, currently valued at £7,500. However, such an award is not triggered by a still-born child, even if the still-birth was the consequence of negligence.

## Possible future developments

The magnitude of an award of damages – quantum – is often as contentious as the legal basis for the claim. Some cases go to trial solely on this issue, even when liability has been determined or acknowledged. Even in cases resolved by negotiation, there is often a very striking difference between the value of the claim as first calculated by the opposing legal teams. Sometimes this reflects a difference of medical opinion on future life expectancy but usually also includes major differences in the assessment of individual loss, need and the cost of providing for it. Here too expert opinion is obtained from diverse care therapists, employment experts and forensic accountants. Much time, effort and legal expense are then invested in resolving the differences.

Several changes have been proposed to reduce this conflict. One is the use of single, jointly-instructed or even court-appointed experts to advise on matters of quantum. Another is to define a set of guidelines for the care consequences and costs of specific injuries. Yet another possibility is to define and compensate immediate need and thereafter provide an annuity to cover need for the duration of the claimant's lifetime, so avoiding calculations based upon a tenuous assessment of prognosis for conditions where the standards and outcome of medical care are changing rapidly. Another source of conflict is the proposal to rescind the statutory provision[4] which permits the costs of future medical treatment to be obtained privately without reference to availability on the NHS. Inevitably there are protagonists and antagonists for all these developments. All that can be said is that maintenance of the *status quo* is unlikely.

## References

1. Kralj v McGrath [1986] 1 All ER 54.
   Attempted cephalic version of a second twin without general anaesthesia. Aggravated damages deemed wholly inappropriate in action brought in negligence and breach of contract. Compensatory damages to be increased instead.
2. Heil v Rankin. *The Times* 24 March 2000 and [2000] Lloyd's Rep Med 203.
   One of 8 test cases, 3 derived from actions in clinical negligence, heard together by the Court of Appeal. General damages should not be increased for awards below £10,000 but above this threshold there should be a tapered increased to a maximum of one third in awards for the most catastrophic injuries.
3. Wells v Wells [1999] 1 AC 345.
   House of Lords decision establishing 3% as the guideline discount rate for calculating future losses.
4. Law Reform (Personal Injuries) Act 1948, s2(4).
   In calculating medical expenses, the possibility of using facilities under the NHS Acts is to be disregarded.

# ▶5

# Legal procedure; the Woolf reforms; role of expert witnesses

New civil procedure rules came into force in April 1999, based upon Lord Woolf's report into civil justice[1]. They represent a radical reform of the legal process, intended to

▶ achieve a just result

▶ treat litigants fairly

▶ offer appropriate procedures at reasonable cost

▶ avoid delay

▶ be understandable and responsive to the needs of users

▶ offer a predictable, effective service, adequately resourced and organised.

The rules apply to both County Court and High Court actions. Terminology has been simplified and unified and a number of familiar terms have been abandoned. The new terminology is used throughout this chapter, with some well-known but now archaic terms included in parentheses. Also in parentheses where appropriate are explanations for the meaning of some legal terms.

## Choice of court

Claims for personal injury, including clinical negligence, are started in the County Court if valued at less than £50,000. Claims of higher value can be started in either the County Court or the High Court. Many, but not all, clinical negligence claims valued at more than £50,000 are started in the High Court because value, complexity or general importance are deemed to warrant the deliberations of a High Court Judge. Designated clinical negligence trial centres, with judges specifically trained and experienced in medical law, are planned as part of the Woolf reforms.

*Appeals* from final orders in the County Court or High Court are heard by the Court of Appeal, composed of three Lord Justices. Appeals are never undertaken lightly and the burden is on the appellant to show that the judge at first instance has erred. Errors of law or principle will be explored far more readily than questions of fact or discretion which are only rarely over-turned. In part this reflects the opportunity for the judge at first instance to hear evidence directly from the witnesses, whereas the Court of Appeal deals solely with the transcript.

*Final appeals* reach the House of Lords and are subject to obtaining leave to appeal, either from the Court of Appeal or House of Lords itself. Matters of exceptional significance are heard by a court of five Law Lords, lesser matters being dealt with by a court of three. Appeal to the House of Lords in clinical negligence claims is infrequent and is used most often as a means of clarifying an important principle or determining legal policy on controversial ethical issues[2,3].

## Commencement of proceedings

A pre-action procedure is now mandatory for claims in both personal injury and clinical negligence. An account of the clinical negligence pre-action protocol is given in chapter 6.

The formal start of a court action is the 'issue' of proceedings. A claim form (formerly a writ or summons) and fee are submitted to the court which then registers the claim, allocates a unique case number and date-stamps the form. It is preferable but not mandatory for particulars of claim (statement of claim in former High Court actions) to be prepared at the same time. The claim form must be 'served' (ie delivered to, by a legally acceptable route) on the defendant or his legal representative (eg hospital solicitor or medical defence organisation) within four months of issue. In practical terms, the particulars of claim are more important than the claim form because they set out the factual basis for the claim, the allegations of breach of duty and of consequential injury. A medical report substantiating the injury and its consequences ('condition and prognosis report') should be served at the same time as the particulars, together with a schedule of special damages (see chapter 4). The claim form, particulars and report should each incorporate a statement of truth. This is a declaration that the party submitting the document believes the facts stated in it are true; a false declaration, made without honest belief in its truth, amounts to contempt of court. Although the claimant's solicitor often makes the declaration on both claim form and particulars, the attestation is to the *claimant's* belief in the factual veracity of the document.

# Responding to a claim

It is incumbent upon a defendant either to file an admission, prepare and serve a defence, or file an acknowledgment of service within 14 days of service of the particulars of claim. Provided service has been acknowledged within 14 days, the defendant has up to 28 days from service of the particulars of claim in which to serve the defence. The parties can agree for this period to be extended for up to 28 days. However, now that the courts rather than the parties have control over the pace of litigation, any agreement to extend the time for service of the defence must be notified to the court in writing.

The defence must state which facts and allegations are

▶ admitted

▶ denied

▶ not admitted – ie require to be proved.

Allegations not specifically answered in one of these three ways are deemed to be admitted.

*Limitation* is a procedural device for denying liability when the claim has been brought out of time. The Limitation Act 1980 requires that actions for personal injury must be started either

▶ within three years from the date of accrual of the cause of action (ie the negligent event)

▶ or within three years of the date of knowledge.

Claims arising from death must be brought within three years of the date of death or three years from the date the claimant or representative first had knowledge.

Date of knowledge is defined as the date on which the claimant first had knowledge

▶ of the identity of the defendant *and*

▶ that the injury was significant *and*

▶ was attributable in whole or in part to the act or omission alleged to be negligent.

Knowledge that the defendant's conduct *is* actionable, as a matter of law, is not required.

The three year period does not operate against persons 'under a disability'. The term refers to children below 18 years, and those of unsound mind, sometimes referred to as 'patients'. A person is of unsound mind if, by reason of a mental disorder within the meaning of the Mental Health Act 1983, he is incapable of managing and administering his property and affairs. The three-year period begins to run against a youthful claimant when he reaches the age of 18 years. Those of unsound mind either at the time of the incident or as a result of it, are not subject to limitation unless they recover their faculties. The Limitation Act also provides a discretionary power which can allow a case to continue, despite a prolonged lapse of time. Trial of limitation as a preliminary point may then be needed, either before, or at the start of, the trial of the action.

A feature of the new procedural rules is the requirement for the defence to include *reasons* for denial of facts or allegations. Formerly a 'holding defence' was acceptable – a legal device for saying nothing relevant and buying time, for example: "If, which is not admitted, the plaintiff suffered a cardiac arrest, it is denied that the same was caused by the negligence of the defendant as alleged or at all". This unhelpful and uninformative response was perceived by patients as denial by the *doctor*, not as part of legal manoeuvring, so adding a sense of insult to injury and evoking angry claims of doctors closing rank, wilful obfuscation and so on. The requirement today is for a defence which sets out the defendant's explanation for what occurred, incorporating if necessary a rebuttal of the claimant's medical report and/or schedule. Finally the defence too must now include a statement of truth by or on behalf of practitioner or trust.

Further legal exchanges may then follow between the parties – formulation of a reply to the defence, or a request for further information (formerly a request for further and better particulars) or specific questions (interrogatories) directed to identified individuals. The totality of this formal documentation constitutes the statement of case (pleadings).

## Subsequent conduct

Once the defence has been filed (ie received by the court), the parties are required to co-operate with the court to ensure proper allocation of the claim to a particular legal 'track', usually the multi-track for clinical negligence claims. Thereafter they follow the court's instructions relating to such matters as exchange of witness statements (ie witnesses of fact – the claimant/ patient and clinical staff involved in the incident), disclosure of documents, exchange of expert reports and the setting of a trial time-table. Only very few clinical negligence claims reach trial. Most are either settled by negotiation or are discontinued by the claimant. The new rules permit either party to make an offer ('Part 36 offer') to settle on specific terms. Significant cost penalties are incurred if an offer is refused but that party subsequently does less well at trial, a provision which provides a powerful incentive to make or accept carefully considered proposals.

A number of cases are settled without a formal admission of liability, although lay persons, particularly patient and practitioner, are likely to interpret such an outcome as tantamount to an admission. Economic expediency is also taken into consideration, particularly when the value of the claim is of low by comparison with the costs of trial. There is good reason for this. The general rule is that a successful party recovers its costs from the losing party, but claimants assisted by Legal Aid (currently the majority) are an exception. Thus even a successful defence is costly for the trust, the NHSLA (see chapter 7) or medical defence organisation. There are obvious conflicts between the competing requirements to conserve scarce financial resources, preserve the professional reputation of hospitals and practitioners, and present a robust defence, when appropriate, to ensure claims in medical negligence are not perceived as an easy route to securing compensation. Erosion of the independent legal status of hospital medical staff by the introduction of NHS indemnity (see chapter 2) has exacerbated practitioners' sense of personal reputation sacrificed for financial advantage. A better view is to recognise that Legal Aid is rarely continued for cases which do not have at least an arguable chance of succeeding and that liability is often a matter of corporate rather than individual responsibility, in other words, a system error[4].

## The role of the expert witness

Professional opinion provides the foundation for judicial determination of both breach of duty and causation of injury. If it is to be of value in reaching a just outcome, it must be accurate, up to date, comprehensive, objective and non-partisan. Such idealism has not always been realised. Judicial recommendations for the role of experts[5] ante-date Lord Woolf's report but had not made a significant impact. In the new procedural rules, the role of the expert is very clearly defined:

▶ the expert's duty is to the court and overrides his duty to the party instructing him

▶ the report must be addressed to the court and

▶ contain a statement confirming the expert understands and has complied with this duty

- the expert must state the substance of all material instructions given to him

- give details of his qualifications and those of any person assisting with tests carried out

- give details of learned literature on which he has relied in formulating his opinion

- summarise the *range* of medical opinion and give reasons for reaching his own opinion

- verify his report with a statement of truth.

The courts have been given far greater power over expert evidence by the new rules. It cannot be adduced at all without leave of the court and its use, particularly oral testimony, is to be restricted to that which is reasonably required to resolve the proceedings. The court can direct that evidence on an issue be given by a single expert and, if the parties cannot agree on a nominee, can select the expert or appoint an assessor to assist. The court can, and often does, direct that there be a meeting of experts requiring them to identify the issues and, if possible, agree some or all of them. Alternatively the court can specify which issues are to be discussed, and require the experts to prepare a joint statement setting out any matters on which they agree, those on which they disagree and why. Written questions to the opposing expert are also permitted.

Concern has been expressed that authoritative experts will over-rule more timid colleagues, that decision-making has been handed back to the medical profession, and that reliance on single experts is wholly inappropriate in matters of breach of duty and often on causation too. Some protection is afforded by careful construction of the agenda for experts' meetings, preferably with medical input, and incorporating as far as possible questions which require only a 'yes' or 'no' answer. Furthermore, parties are not legally bound by an agreement reached by experts, unless they agree to be bound. The court retains the power to act as final arbiter. Some commentators argue for the presence of both parties' legal advisers at the meeting of experts whereas others consider more fruitful discussion will take place in their absence. Final recommendations on the conduct of such meetings are being formulated and are likely to evolve with experience.

## References

1. Access to Justice. Final report by The Right Honourable the Lord Woolf MR to the Lord Chancellor on the civil justice system in England and Wales. HMSO, July 1996.

Actions in medical negligence singled out as the area where civil justice failed most conspicuously. Reasons included disproportion between costs and damages, particularly in low value cases, a low rate of success, excessive delay, prolonged unwarranted pursuit of unmeritorious claims or indefensible defences, and more intense suspicion and lack of co-operation between the parties than in many other areas of litigation. A damning commentary!

2. Gillick v W Norfolk & Wisbech AHA [1986] AC 112.

An issue of social principle: is it acceptable to provide contraceptive advice to a child below 16 years without parental consent? Decision of the House of Lords forms the basis for defining the consensual capacity of children.

3. Airedale NHS Trust v Bland [1993] 4 Med LR 39.

Validity of withdrawing life-sustaining treatment from a patient in persistent vegetative state. House of Lords was careful to point out that each case should be considered individually – policy was a matter for parliament.

4. Reason J. Human error: models and management. BMJ 2000 320:768-70.

Psychologist's account of the sources of human error – the person approach and the system approach.

5. The 'Ikarian Reefer' [1993] 2 Lloyd's Rep 68.

Judicial analysis of the role and duties of expert witnesses, in this case in a maritime context. Many of the recommendations made by Cresswell J are now incorporated in Part 35 of the Civil Procedural Rules.

# ▶6

# Pre-action protocol; alternative dispute resolution

The pre-action stage of litigation was identified by Lord Woolf[1] as a major source of cost and delay in the conduct of claims arising from alleged clinical negligence. He recommended the development of a pre-action protocol to foster the co-operative resolution of disputes between patients and health care providers rather than immediate resort to litigation. The Clinical Disputes Forum[2] was established as a result of his suggestion that an 'umbrella group', representing the interests of all those involved in clinical negligence claims, should be set up to pursue this objective. The Pre-Action Protocol, now incorporated into the Civil Procedure Rules, was its first achievement. In the foreword, Lord Irvine LC described protocols as "the first serious attempt to set effective and enforceable standards for the efficient conduct of pre-action litigation".

## The Clinical Negligence Pre-Action Protocol

The purpose of the protocol is to

▶ maintain or restore the relationship between patient and health care provider

▶ resolve as many disputes as possible without litigation.

It seeks to do so by means of

▶ openness – early, reciprocal, communication

▶ timeliness – of investigation, response and appraisal of merit

▶ consideration – of all available options for resolution.

There are three essential steps:

▶ disclosure of medical records

▶ letter of claim

▶ response to the letter of claim.

## Disclosure of medical records

A request for records should provide sufficient information to alert the trust or practitioner to the nature and magnitude of the adverse outcome, and specify, as far as possible, which records are required. Use of a standard form is recommended. Copy records should be provided within 40 days of the request, and explanation offered promptly if there are genuine reasons why this target cannot be met. Disclosure should be voluntary – it can in any case be enforced by the courts or sought by the patient under the terms of the Access to Health Records Act 1990. Disclosure of sensitive additional information such as internal audit reports is considered in chapter 8.

## The Letter of Claim

This letter is based upon initial expert opinion obtained to assess whether the claimant has grounds for seeking redress. Prepared by the claimant's legal advisers, it sets out the basis for the claim in formal but non-legalistic terms. It should include

▶ a summary of the facts, with a chronology if appropriate

▶ the allegations of breach of duty

▶ the harm which is alleged to have been caused as a result

▶ an indication of the value of the claim.

The claimant (ie his legal advisers) may elect to disclose expert evidence at this stage and is expected to do so if combining the letter of claim with an offer to settle (see chapter 5).

A letter of claim is not deemed to be legally binding and, if the matter proceeds to litigation, discrepancies may be detected between it and subsequent pleadings. Similarly the assessment of financial loss may be no more than preliminary, particularly in complex, high-value claims.

## Response to the letter of claim

The letter of claim should be acknowledged within 14 days of receipt and should name the individual responsible for handling subsequent correspondence. The letter of response should follow within three months of the letter of claim and should include

- what, if any, part of the claim is admitted
- what allegations are denied
- reasoned argument for the denial
- factual commentary or chronology if the claimant's version is disputed.

If an offer to settle has been made, the defendant should respond to the offer, with reasons for the stance adopted. A counter-offer can be made, with expert evidence adduced in support. Evidence refuting breach of duty can also usefully be disclosed – eg protocols or guidelines.

## Resolution without legal proceedings

The steps outlined above may suffice to permit settlement of a proportion of claims by negotiation, usually between the claimant's solicitor and either an experienced Claims Manager, the trust's solicitors or a medical defence organisation. The role of the NHSLA in settlement of claims above a threshold figure is discussed in chapter 7. If there is a risk that the claimant's position may be compromised by delay since the allegedly negligent event (see Limitation in chapter 5), formal legal action may be commenced by the issue but not service of proceedings. The maximum permitted interval between issue and service (four months) exceeds the time allowed for responding to a letter of claim (three months). It should therefore never be necessary for legal proceedings to be served without first conforming with the pre-action protocol.

## Alternative dispute resolution (ADR)

This is a generic term encompassing all methods for reaching settlement other than litigation.

*Arbitration* is rarely used in clinical claims. It is consensual in that issues are determined by a nominated or agreed arbitrator who is conversant with the subject of dispute. The conduct of the arbitration is adversarial, cases being presented by counsel and supported by expert evidence in a manner similar to trial. It is used most often in commercial disputes arising from contract.

*Mediation* is also a consensual procedure in which the parties must agree not only to proceed to mediation, but must also agree the terms of any settlement reached before they are bound by it. The mediator is usually recruited from a professional agency and, having been sent documents outlining the basis for the claim and its defence, convenes a meeting attended by both parties and their solicitors. In a common forum, both parties summarise the essential elements of their case and then they disperse, each party with advisers to a separate room. The mediator then enters discussions with each party in turn, exploring what their hopes and expectations are, what features are seen as essential elements of any settlement, what awareness each side has of weaknesses in its case. Knowledge acquired by the mediator is confidential unless permission is given to relay it to the other side. Unlike a litigated settlement, mediation can encompass elements of redress other than financial compensation – an apology, explanation, commitment to a particular course of action by the trust or on behalf of a named individual. The process is confidential, fosters co-operation, and has the potential to disperse emotion, re-establish confidence and restore easy communication between doctor and patient. Solutions cannot be imposed. The role of the mediator is purely to *assist the parties* to reach an agreed settlement.

The **NHS mediation pilot study**[3] sought to identify the potential for mediating claims in clinical negligence. Take-up was disappointingly low but cases which were mediated usually reached settlement and most participants expressed satisfaction with the process. Reluctance to embark on mediation was apparent among both claimants and defendants – a finding echoed in the civil courts in general. Reasons for this reluctance are neither obvious nor always valid. Ignorance of the procedure, fear that control will be lost and concern that inappropriately low financial settlements may be agreed all contribute. However, there is a now climate of change. Mediation was specifically recommended by a Commons Select Health Committee Report on adverse clinical incidents[4], has been rendered more attractive by changes in funding policy, and can be required by the courts, possibly even as a pre-requisite to the commencement of legal proceedings.

*Other techniques of alternative dispute resolution* such as early neutral evaluation or expert determination have not been explored in the context of claims arising from clinical practice.

## References

1. Access to justice. Final report on the civil justice system in England and Wales by The Right Honourable the Lord Woolf MR. HMSO July 1996.
   Lord Woolf's comments on medical negligence are summarised in preceding chapter under reference 1.
2. Clinical Disputes Forum. Information is available at www.clinical-disputes-forum.org.uk
   A voluntary, multi-disciplinary body set up in 1997 to promote less adversarial and more cost effective ways of resolving disputes about healthcare and medical treatment.

3. Mulcahy L. Mediating Medical Negligence Claims: an option for the future? HMSO, January 2000.

   Final report on the NHS mediation pilot study.

4. Sixth Report of the House of Commons Select Committee: Procedures related to adverse clinical incidents and outcomes in medical care. HMSO November 1999.

   At paragraph 130, the Committee recommends 'that the Government reviews, clarifies and improves the funding, and other, arrangements relating to mediation and acts on the findings of the pilot mediation scheme.'

# ▶7
# Funding litigation

Litigation is costly. Claims in clinical negligence are among the most expensive, not least because expert evidence is so often required on all three aspects – breach of duty, causation of injury and quantum. It is common for costs to exceed the value of the claim when damages are less than £10,000. A significant proportion of these costs is incurred before it is possible to predict with any accuracy whether or not the claimant has reasonable prospects of success. If initial investigation suggests there are no grounds for further pursuit, the expenditure has all been in vain. If the prospects for success are equivocal, the claimant is tempted to continue but is then at risk of an adverse outcome at trial. A successful defendant can recoup the expense of defending the claim from an unsuccessful claimant who, if privately funded, is then responsible for the expenses incurred by both parties. Few patients are prepared to take such risks.

## Legal Aid *(provisions before April 1 2000)*

Legal Aid was introduced in 1949 to assist those otherwise unable to afford legal advice, assistance or representation. The benefit is means tested, those with some resources being required to contribute on a regular basis as the claim evolves. Children can obtain legal aid in their own name without reference to the resources of their parents. If a legally-aided action is lost, contributions made by the individual cannot be recovered and the Legal Aid Board suffers a loss. Conversely, the successful claimant can expect to recoup costs from the defendant sufficient to reimburse expenditure by the Board and most if not all his own contribution. A successful defendant however cannot, as general rule, recover costs from a legally-aided party.

These rules put the legally-aided claimant in a very strong financial position for as long as legal aid is continued. The defendant faced by a legally-aided claimant is bound to suffer financially – by paying both sides' costs if the defence fails or at least own costs if successful. This financial predicament is a powerful incentive to out-of-court settlement which avoids the expense of trial. The grant of legal aid is subject to review as the case proceeds and will be withdrawn unless the Legal Aid Board is satisfied the case has at least a reasonable chance of success and is worthy of continued assistance – largely an estimate of cost-effectiveness. Despite this requirement the perception among defendants has been of limitless support for unmeritorious cases.

Regulations brought into force in 1999 restrict the handling of legally-aided claims in clinical negligence to solicitors who are able, by demonstrating experience in this field, to secure a clinical negligence franchise contract with the Legal Aid Board. This innovation is intended to ensure that claimants obtain efficient services and funds are deployed wisely.

## Legal Services Commission *(provisions after April 1 2000)*

This new body, established by the Access to Justice Act 1999, replaces the Legal Aid Board from April 1st 2000. Financial assistance will be available thereafter from the Community Legal Service Fund according to new priorities set out in the legislation. Most personal injury and fatal accident claims are excluded. If financial assistance is required for their pursuit, this should be arranged on the basis of a conditional fee agreement. Claims for personal injury arising from clinical negligence are excepted from this rule and will continue to be funded, and to be handled only by solicitors holding a clinical negligence franchise. The retention of public funding for clinical negligence claims reflects in part the high cost of insurance premiums to cover conditional fee agreements in an area notorious for unpredictability of outcome and high litigation costs. However, new regulations are introduced which will restrict financial assistance according to the estimated prospect for success and the ratio between damages and likely costs. These measures are intended to weed out cases unlikely to succeed and those with costs disproportionate to value.

## Conditional fee agreements (CFA's)

A conditional fee agreement permits solicitors and counsel to enter into a contract with the claimant which provides for fees to be paid only if the case succeeds. A percentage uplift ('success fee') of up to 100% of the basic fee can also be charged in successful cases. The claimant's costs, the success fee and the premium for any insurance arranged to cover possible liability for the costs of a successful defendant, can all be recovered by a successful claimant. The unsuccessful claimant will sacrifice any insurance premium, and the unsuccessful legal team will remain unpaid. The claimant's lawyers however are *not* responsible for the costs of a successful defendant, even if the ligitant has pursued the claim under a CFA without insurance cover[1]. Insurance is not an obligatory element of a CFA and a number of claimants are insured for legal expenses in any event through household or other policies. An anticipated benefit of CFA's is a reduction in prolonged, unwarranted legal advice to pursue unmeritorious claims.

## Funding the defence of clinical negligence claims

The escalating volume and value of claims for medical negligence during the 1980's led to a rapid rise in premiums for professional indemnity, a problem resolved for practitioners employed within NHS hospitals by the advent of NHS indemnity in 1990[2]. However, this provides *only* for claims arising from events occurring within the course of the practitioner's employment.

The role of the *medical defence organisations (MDO's)* has changed as a result. While continuing to provide support and assistance to their members, they no longer have any financial responsibility for actions brought against trusts and have no control over the conduct of the litigation. They retain both control and financial responsibility for actions brought against insured general practitioners, those engaged in private practice and overseas members.

In April 1995, the *Clinical Negligence Scheme for Trusts (CNST)* was introduced as a means of pooling the cost of successful claims against NHS trusts. Membership is voluntary but virtually all trusts have elected to subscribe. Premiums are determined according to the efficacy of risk-management strategies as judged against criteria established by the CNST at its inception. A scheme to cover liability for claims arising before April 1995 – the *Existing Liabilities Scheme (ELS)* – was established in 1996. It is available for claims in excess of £10,000, provided certain management criteria are fulfilled, and is independent of membership of CNST. 80% of costs between £10,000 and £500,000 and all costs above £500,000 can be recouped under ELS.

In November 1995, the *National Health Service Litigation Authority (NHSLA)* was established as a special health authority with responsibility for administering the clinical negligence scheme for trusts and, later, the existing liabilities scheme too. The authority also has a remit to sustain or improve patient care, to ensure that patients have access to appropriate remedies and recompense, and that claims handling is carried out consistently, efficiently and cost-effectively[3]. Since April 1999, the role of the NHSLA has been expanded to include responsibility for non-clinical litigation against trusts. Clinical claims above a threshold selected by the trust (from £10,000 – £100,000) must be notified to the NHSLA and handled by one of a designated panel of solicitors. Claims below the threshold can still be handled locally. The trust is responsible for payments up to its threshold on every claim, and for 80% of payments between the threshold and a predetermined maximum above which all expenditure is covered by the NHSLA.

## References

1. Hodgson v Imperial Tobacco Ltd [1998] 2 All ER 673.
   Court of Appeal ruling that lawyers acting under conditional fee arrangements on behalf of unsuccessful, uninsured claimants are not responsible for the costs of the successful defendant.
2. Claims of medical negligence against NHS hospital and community doctors and dentists. Department of Health Circular 1989: HC (89) 34.
   Health Circular published in 1989 setting out arrangements for NHS indemnity to apply from January 1 1990. Authorities could no longer *require* employed staff to subscribe to a recognised professional defence organisation but should encourage staff to ensure they have 'adequate defence cover as appropriate'.
3. The National Health Service Litigation Authority Framework Document. Department of Health, September 1996.
   Sets out aims, objectives and functions of the NHSLA and how it relates to Ministers and the NHS Executive.

# ►8
# Confidentiality and disclosure; inquests, inquiries and internal audit

Health care rarely spawns legal claims founded on breach of confidentiality. The requirements if such a claim is to succeed are that

► the information must have the necessary quality of confidence

► it must have been imparted in circumstances importing an obligation of confidence

► unauthorised use of the information has caused detriment to the party imparting it.

Medical records are confidential documents and should not be released to any third party without the consent of the patient. This rule can be waived in some circumstances, for example, if disclosure is required by statute (notifiable diseases), or the safety of the public or an identified individual is at risk[1]. Many of the exceptions are a matter of professional discretion rather than of law[2], the guiding principle being that the practitioner must give good reason for disclosure.

## Disclosure of medical records in the context of litigation

*Voluntary disclosure* of case notes to a patient's solicitor requires the written consent of the patient or representative. This is so whether the records sought are the property of a potential defendant or an uninvolved practitioner or trust. The claimant's express authority is *not* required for disclosure to the trust or practitioner's legal advisers when a patient intimates an intention to take action against them. Either confidentiality is deemed to have been waived or it can be argued that disclosure is in the public interest to ensure prompt, efficient and just disposal of the case.

*Compulsory disclosure* can be enforced by court order against a potential defendant before an action begins, or against an uninvolved third party after proceedings have commenced. Practitioners can also be summoned to attend court, either to give oral evidence of matters within their knowledge or to produce documentation within their control. They are obliged to attend and only exceptionally might a judge exercise discretion and disallow sensitive questioning.

The *Access to Health Records Act 1990* applies to records made after November 1 1991. It provides patients or their legal representatives with

▶ a right of access to their own medical notes

▶ a right to challenge or seek correction for inaccuracies.

Notes to which the Act applies are those made by a health professional *in connection with the care of the individual*. Entries before November 1 1991 may also be disclosed if the record-holder deems this necessary for the understanding of later records. Disclosure must be made within 40 days and explanation must be made available for 'unintelligible entries'. If a death has occurred, disclosure can be sought not only on behalf of the estate but also by 'any person who may have a claim arising from the death', unless there is written evidence that such disclosure would be contrary to the wishes of the deceased. Most requests are made by a solicitor and require written authority from the person in whom the right is vested.

There are a number of exceptions to the right to disclosure under the Act, most importantly:

▶ if the record-holder believes disclosure is likely to cause serious harm to the physical or mental health of the patient or any other person

▶ the information relates to, or has been provided by, a person other than the patient (or a health care professional) who could be identified from the records and who has not consented to the disclosure.

The consequence of this legislation is that the potential litigant can, in most cases, obtain disclosure more easily than by reliance on a court order and, at the outset, can obtain possibly relevant records from an uninvolved hospital or practitioner. However the extent of disclosure made under the Act is arguably more restricted than can be ordered by the court on individual application. For example, an audit report affecting an individual is not part of the 'health record' but could be sought by application to the court for specific discovery. The practical consequence of access authorised by statute is that disclosure of medical and nursing notes is now usually made voluntarily. Most disputes centre on release of records of patients with mental illness[3].

# The *Data Protection Acts 1984 and 1998*

The first of these Acts provided a right of access for patients to computerised information held about them, subject to exceptions similar to those outlined above for the Access to Health Records Act. The 1998 Act extends this right of access to manually held records.

The *Human Rights Act 1998* includes a right to freedom of expression but confirms a responsibility to prevent disclosure of information imparted in confidence.

# Disclosure in specific circumstances

*Loss or destruction of records* – including X-rays and charts – is likely to be interpreted to the disadvantage of the record-holder, even if wholly innocent. This is particularly so if records are destroyed when it is already clear that legal proceedings are in contemplation[4].

*Inquiries and internal audit reports* often contain sensitive information and may identify errors of procedure or their implementation. Audit which identifies individual patients is 'confidential' and should be treated as such. Anonymised data is preferred if wider disclosure is required to prompt system changes. Reports prepared in contemplation of litigation are 'privileged' – in other words, immune from disclosure. However, litigation as the sole or prime purpose *at the time of preparation* is the cardinal requirement. A confidential accident report, prepared in accordance with an NHS Circular, dealt not only with possible litigation but also considered if action was needed to prevent repetition. Disclosure was ordered on the grounds that the second purpose was at least as important as the first[5]. In another case, privilege in a report prepared solely in contemplation of litigation was deemed to have been waived when it was disclosed to an expert who then made reference to it in his own report[6]. Alternatively the Judge was prepared to exercise his discretion in favour of disclosure. There is no judicial *authority* for a duty of candour resting on professional staff in the context of actions in professional negligence, but the concept is widely and increasingly endorsed. Concerns that a finding of negligence is inevitable, if a report advocating system change after an adverse incident is disclosed, are unfounded. Negligence is determined by the standards which pertained at the time of the incident: being wise after the event is not necessarily indicative of poor practice.

The *results of research* can be published or disclosed without breach of confidentiality *provided* individual patients cannot be identified[7].

Conversely, non-consensual publication of a case report in a specialist journal, which allowed a practitioner to identify herself, was unacceptable.

*Disclosure of medical records at or before an inquest* is sometimes requested either by the coroner or by the relatives of the deceased. The Access to Health Records Act 1990 provides for disclosure to a deceased's personal representative or any person who may have a claim arising from the patient's death. The court can also order disclosure of medical notes in favour of the same persons before an inquest but only for the sole purpose of ascertaining the cause of death[8]. It is doubtful if the coroner has a *power* to secure disclosure of notes before the inquest. However he is required to examine, on oath, all persons having knowledge as to the facts of the death whom he considers it expedient to examine, can issue a subpoena requiring attendance (with penalties for non-compliance) and can impose a fine upon a witness who, without lawful excuse, refuses to answer a question put to him. In view of these provisions, it is hardly surprising that voluntary disclosure of notes to both coroner and family is now usually given on request.

## References

1. W v Egdell [1989] 2 WLR 689.
   Psychiatrist voluntarily disclosed to a mental hospital and the Home Office an unfavourable report on a paranoid schizophrenic, who had been convicted of manslaughter but was, by then, seeking less stringent detention. Public interest in disclosure outweighed W's private interests. In the US case of *Tarasoff v Regents of University of California*, it was held that a psychologist owed a duty of care to a particular woman, murdered by one of his patients who had expressed an intention to kill her. She should have been forewarned, despite breach of confidentiality.
2. Confidentiality. Guidelines of the General Medical Council, 1998.
   Statement amplifying the recommendations of *Good Medical Practice*, July 1998.
3. R v Mid-Glamorgan FHSA *ex parte* Martin [1994] 5 Med LR 383.
   Schizophrenic patient sought disclosure of medical records pre-dating operation of Access to Health Records Act. Court of Appeal held there was no common law right of access and claimant was excluded by the terms of the Act.
4. Hammond v W Lancs HA [1998] Lloyd's Rep Med 146.
   X-rays destroyed, despite receipt of a letter before action, because hospital did not consider they were part of a patient's medical records, a view regarded by the judge as 'wholly unacceptable'.
5. Lask v Gloucester HA [1991] 2 Med LR 379.
   Accident report prepared after patient fell in hospital grounds. NHS Circular (55)66 identifies purpose as preparation for litigation *and* measures to prevent repetition. Disclosure of the accident report was ordered.
6. Clough v Tameside & Glossop HA [1998] Lloyd's Rep Med 69.
   Claim arising from birth of child with Down's syndrome after alleged failure to accede to a request for amniocentesis. Report prepared, at request of MDU, by an SHO involved in antenatal care, was relayed to psychiatrist instructed on behalf of the hospital to provide expert comment on magnitude of plaintiff's psychiatric injury. Psychiatrist alluded to the SHO's report and, when psychiatric evidence was disclosed, plaintiff sought and obtained SHO's report.
7. R v Department of Health *ex parte* Source Informatics Ltd [2000] Lloyd's Rep Med 76.
   Court of Appeal decision permitting disclosure, for commercial purposes, of anonymised

prescription data. Issue deemed to be of such importance that representation and intervention in the appeal were allowed on behalf of the GMC, MRC, ABPI and the National Pharmaceutical Association.

8. **Stobart v Nottingham HA [1992] 3 Med LR 284.**

Discovery of medical records before an inquest deemed to lie within Supreme Court Rules for pre-action disclosure. Ascertainment or attempts to ascertain the cause of death ... not a collateral purpose but well within the reasons for granting discovery. However, any attempt to go beyond the one issue (ie cause of death) would not be permissible.

# ►9

# Consent; minors and the mentally incapacitated; research; training

Intentional, non-consensual touching is a tort (battery) or, if carried out in anger, a criminal offence. Unlike actions founded in negligence, claims for battery do not need to prove that injury has occurred as a result – the mere fact of non-consensual touching is sufficient to establish liability. However, attempts to bring actions for battery claiming invalid consent to medical treatment rarely succeed[1], provided the claimant has consented in general terms[2]. Claims founded on alleged insufficiency of information rendering consent invalid are brought in negligence, not battery, and so proof of consequential injury is necessary if the claim is to succeed.

## What constitutes valid consent?

Consent to treatment is only valid if the patient is

▶ competent to take the decision

▶ provided with sufficient information

▶ acts voluntarily.

*Competence* to take the decision[3] requires the ability

▶ to understand information given

▶ to retain and believe it, and

▶ to use it to reach a reasoned decision.

## The nature of consent

*Implied consent* is the basis for many diagnostic or therapeutic interventions, eg physical examination or venepuncture. *Express written consent* is preferred for procedures which are more than minimally invasive, require general anaesthesia or are associated with significant risk. The fact that a consent form has been signed is evidence only that the patient has consented to the procedure, *not* proof that the consent is necessarily valid (eg adequately informed).

The ***doctrine of necessity*** is the basis for assuming consent when urgent, life-saving treatment is deemed necessary but the patient is unable to provide valid consent. It extends only to those measures which are required immediately. Non-urgent treatment which a practitioner considers advisable (ie in the patient's best interests), or more conveniently carried out at the same time, is not covered and, if performed, may prompt disciplinary proceedings and/or a claim for damages[4].

## Was consent given voluntarily?

This is rarely a cause of conflict but has sufficed to persuade the court to authorise blood transfusion to a former Jehovah's witness whose written declaration against such treatment, made while still legally competent, was held to have been the consequence of parental pressure[5]. An unsuccessful action by parents of a child brain damaged after cardiac transplantation[6] alleged they were given insufficient information about risk and were also pressurised into giving consent.

## What constitutes 'sufficient information'?

Sufficiency of information is still defined at English law by the *Bolam* principle – judicial appraisal of professional opinon[7] – whereas in other jurisdictions the court determines what suffices[8]. However an increasingly prescriptive approach can be expected in the English courts following recently published *professional* guidelines[9,10] which advocate a more rigidly defined standard of disclosure than mere reliance on currently accepted practice.

Claimants bringing an action founded on the allegation that consent was invalidated because the information given fell below an acceptable standard, must be able to show

▶ that the information given was, in fact, inadequate by accepted standards *and*

▶ consent would have been withheld had the proper information been supplied.

Inevitably such actions are only brought when there has been an adverse outcome. It is often difficult for the claimant to satisfy the court on the second limb of the test if the risk which materialised was infrequent, and worthwhile benefit was anticipated from the treatment[11].

## Who is entitled to consent or withhold consent to medical treatment?

Adult patients are assumed to be competent to consent to treatment in the absence of evidence to the contrary. They may withhold consent, even to life-saving treatment[5], and can do so by means of an 'advance directive' provided the decision was made when the patient was

- demonstrably competent

- acting voluntarily and

- the decision covers the circumstances which prevail when treatment is contemplated.

Assessing competence may require independent psychiatric advice if time and opportunity allow. There are no clear guidelines on the proper course of action if, during a procedure for which consent has been properly obtained, a patient requests that it be terminated. In a Canadian case[12] it was held that continued validity of consent is a matter for the exercise of medical judgment.

## Consent by or on behalf of children

Section 8 of the Family Law Reform Act 1969 entitles children aged 16 to 18 years to give valid consent to surgical, medical or dental *treatment* without the involvement of parent or guardian. It does not cover the donation of organs, blood or participation in research, nor does it permit a child of this age to *refuse* treatment[13]. Parents or guardians can give valid consent to treatment for children up to the age of majority (18 years). The Children Act 1989 permits either parent to consent if they were married when the child was born, or the mother if they were not. Circumstances in which others may consent on behalf of the child are also set out in the Act. If the parent or guardian refuses consent and the practitioner considers this is against the best interests of the child, application can be made for the decision to be over-ruled by the court. Each case is decided on its own merits[14] and the decision is not a foregone conclusion.

Children below the age of 16 years can give valid consent to medical treatment without parental involvement *provided* they have sufficient maturity and intelligence fully to understand the implications of what is proposed[15], a test widely referred to as '*Gillick* competent'. A higher level of maturity and understanding should be sought for more serious procedures. Decisions at this age to refuse recommended treatment should be given due regard but are often over-ruled[16].

## Consent on behalf of the mentally incompetent

Lack of legal competence in the sense defined here can be permanent or transitory. There is currently no legal authority vested in relatives, those holding enduring power of attorney, or even the courts, to consent to treatment on behalf of an incompetent adult[5]. The doctrine of necessity can still be invoked for emergency treatments, and treatment for mental illness (but not coincident physical illness unless a manifestation of the mental illness[17]) can also be given without consent. The Mental Health Act 1983 cannot be invoked to justify treatment or procedures unconnected with the mental condition, even if a patient exhibits apparent irrationality and thoughts contrary to the views of the majority[18]. Only the court can make a declaration as to the lawfulness or otherwise of a proposal to treat a mentally incompetent adult. Treatment without such a declaration is not necessarily 'unlawful', it is merely unprotected by the court. Such a declaration should therefore be sought for contentious proposals such as sterilisation or the withdrawal of supportive treatment[19,20]. The test adopted is that of **best interests**, a concept easy to understand but difficult to define. In the context of a proposal to undertake vasectomy on a man with Down's syndrome, it was held to encompass medical, emotional and all other welfare issues pertaining to the incompetent person[21]. The court declined to comment on whether social considerations or the interests of others should be considered too.

In the absence of a clearly identifiable and accessible source from which to obtain consent on behalf of mentally incompetent adults, patients and practitioners are vulnerable. Legislation is anticipated to permit the appointment of a proxy (medical attorney) to take treatment decisions on behalf of incompetent adults, including proleptic appointment in case of future incompetence. Specific authorisation would be required for power to seek withdrawal of nutrition and hydration.

## Consent for research and teaching

The legal principles of consent apply to research as much as to treatment, whether it be primarily therapeutic (ie with potential to benefit the subject) or non-therapeutic. Widely accepted professional practice[22] recognises that more information needs to be given if the outcome of a proposed procedure is unknown or of no potential value to the individual, but conflict over consent to research has spawned few legal cases. There are no specific legal requirements, although the Medical Research Council, Royal College of Physicians and Association of British Pharmaceutical Industries have offered guidelines. So too has the Department of Health[23] which recommends consultation with local Research Ethics Committees 'in matters relating to the ethics of any proposed research project'. These guidelines would probably be recognised by the court as defining the appropriate standard of professional practice. Note that the Law Commission considered it unlawful to undertake non-therapeutic research on adults incompetent to consent[24]. Particular difficulties are also associated with consent for research on children, and an independent inquiry into the trial of a new technique of assisted ventilation may provide some clarification[25].

Gaining and retaining experience is a necessary part of medical education and it is inevitable that trainees, before or after graduation, will be involved in clinical procedures. Consent is not invalidated provided no commitment has been given that a named practitioner will undertake the treatment. It is the *procedure* to which consent has been given. However, the Department of Health recommends that explicit consent should be obtained for the involvement of students[26]. If some element of the procedure is changed or extended beyond usual practice, merely to permit students to learn or experienced practitioners to maintain their expertise, the 'nature' of what has been agreed (ie consented) has been changed. Separate, specific consent should be obtained.

# References

1. Appleton & Others v Garrett [1997] 8 Med LR 75.
   Unnecessary dental treatment undertaken for financial gain. Negligence was admitted but claimants also succeeded in an action for 'trespass to the person' (which includes battery) and were awarded aggravated damages.
2. Chatterton v Gerson [1987] 1 All ER 257.
   Neurological damage after a phenol nerve block. Patient deemed to have been informed 'in broad terms' of the nature of the procedure: consent was held to be real and action in battery failed.
3. Re C (Refusal of medical treatment) [1994] 1 All ER 819; noted in [1993] 4 Med LR 238.
   Schizophrenic patient detained at Broadmoor successfully sought an injunction prohibiting amputation of his gangrenous leg without express, written consent. Defines criteria of legal competence to refuse life-saving treatment.
4. Dyer C. BMJ 1998 316:955.
   Parents of 10-year old consented to diagnostic cardiac catheterisation but not balloon dilatation. Practitioner acting in perceived best interest of child attempted balloon dilatation with disastrous

consequences. Criticised for exceeding his remit and suspended for 6 months by GMC for professional misconduct.

5. **Re T (Adult: refusal of treatment) [1992] 3 Med LR 306.**

   Court of Appeal decision confirming the right of competent adults to refuse life-saving treatment and establishing criteria for validity of such a decision. See also *Re MB [1997] 8 Med LR 217* – right to refuse Caesarean section.

6. **Poynter v Hillingdon HA BMJ 1997 314:1224.**

   Unsuccessful claim for damages on behalf of child severely brain damaged after pioneering cardiac transplant. Parents alleged inadequate information was given and that they were pressurised to consent despite their hostility in principle to transplantation. Information provided was deemed acceptable by the standards of the time.

7. **Sidaway v Royal Bethlem and Maudsley Hospital [1985] AC 871.**

   Landmark decision by the House of Lords accepting *Bolam* principle – ie professional opinion – as the determinant of how much information is necessary to render consent valid.

8. **Rogers v Whittaker [1992] 4 Med LR 79 (decision of High Court of Australia).**

   Ophthalmic surgery complicated by sympathetic ophthalmia resulting in virtual blindness. Patient had enquired about possible complications and been reassured. *Bolam* principle rejected: it is for the courts to adjudicate on what is an appropriate standard care. Breach of duty is not to be concluded on expert medical evidence alone.

9. **Senate of Surgery of Great Britain and Ireland. The Surgeon's Duty of Care: guidance for surgeons on ethical and legal issues. October 1997.**

   Advocates a 'reasonable patient test' for the giving of information. Also suggests particular needs of the individual should be identified and considered, and surgeon should be satisfied patient has understood the information.

10. **General Medical Council. Seeking patients' consent: the ethical considerations.**

    Published in 1999, it makes similar recommendations to those cited above and states specifically 'existing caselaw gives a guide as to what can be considered *minimum requirements* of good practice'. (Emphasis added)

11. **Smith v Barking, Havering & Brentwood HA [1994] 5 Med LR 285.**

    Unsuccessful action based on alleged failure to give adequate warning. Causation (ie would consent have been withheld if fully informed) to be considered on a subjective basis, but correct to give particular weight to objective assessment unless there are extraneous or additional factors. Can claimant answer reliably after adverse outcome?

12. **Ciarlariello *et al* v Schacter *et al* [1991] 2 Med LR 391. (Court of Appeal, Ontario).**

    During a second cerebral angiogram to locate source of sub-arachnoid haemorrhage, patient insisted test be stopped. It was, and then resumed 10-15 minutes later; quadriplegia followed the final injection. Burden of deciding whether to *commence* the test lay with patient but, once initiated, risk assessment became a matter of medical judgment.

13. **Re J (A Minor) (Medical Treatment [1992] 3 Med LR 317.**

    16 year old with anorexia nervosa. Court has power to over-rule refusal by a minor, even if over 16 years. For procedure see *Re O (A Minor) (Medical Treatment) [1993] 4 Med LR 272* (blood transfusion for premature neonate with RDS; parents Jehovah's witnesses); also *R v Portsmouth Hospital NHS Trust [1999] Lloyd's Rep Med 367*: violent conflict between medical staff and family over decision to withhold treatment from disabled 12-year old.

14. **Re C (A Minor) (Medical Treatment – Refusal of parental consent) [1997] 8 Med LR 166.**

    Parents of infant with biliary atresia, both experienced health care workers, refused consent to liver transplant which had been recommended as in child's best interests by three doctors. Strong presumption in favour of preserving life is not an absolute rule and best interests of child not served by forcing major invasive surgery on devoted mother. Compare *Re B (a minor) [1981] 1 WLR 1421*: surgery ordered for duodenal atresia in infant with Down's syndrome.

15. **Gillick v W Norfolk and Wisbech AHA [1986] AC 112.**

    House of Lords ruling on whether, and in what circumstances, children below 16 years can give valid consent to medical treatment, in this case contraception for a 15 year old; mother intractably hostile to lack of parental input.

16. **Re R (A Minor) [1992] 3 Med LR 342.**
Court of Appeal decision confirming right of parents, guardian or the court to over-rule refusal of treatment by a *'Gillick* competent' adolescent: a psychotic girl aged 15 years 10 months. See also *BMJ 1999 319:209*: cardiac transplantation sanctioned in a 15 year old who refused consent but whose parents had consented. Judge relied upon view formed by *solicitors* interviewing child that her competence had been eroded by illness.

17. **Fox v Riverside Health Trust [1995] 6 Med LR 181.**
Feeding is 'treatment' within s145 of Mental Health Act 1983; forced feeding is 'treatment' for anorexia nervosa.

18. **St George's NHS Trust v S; R v Collins & Others *ex parte* S [1998] 6 Med LR 356.**
Compulsory admission under Mental Health Act used wrongly to over-rule refusal of consent to Caesarean section. Note the unborn child is not 'a person' and does not have rights protected by law.

19. **F v W Berkshire HA [1990] 2 AC 1.**
'Best interests' determine legality of treatment for adult, incompetent patient – in this case, female sterilisation.

20. **Airedale NHS Trust v Bland [1993] 4 Med LR 39.**
Legality of withdrawing treatment from a patient in PVS. Reports from both Court of Appeal and House of Lords.

21. **R-B v Official Solicitor [2000] Lloyd's Rep Med 87.**
Vasectomy for Down's syndrome man not in his best interests, although circumstances could change.

22. **British Medical Association. Medical Ethics Today: its practice and philosophy. BMA Publishing Group, 1993.**
Professional recommendations on consent, including children & research.

23. **Local Research Ethics Committees. Department of Health 1991 HSG (91) 5.**
Department of Health recommendations on conduct of research.

24. **Law Commission Report: Mental Incapacity. 1995 Law Comm 231.**
One of a series of Law Commission Reports on mental incapacity, including comment on research.

25. **Government sets up inquiry into ventilation trial. BMJ 1999 318:553.**
Allegedly inadequate consent for trial of continuous negative extra-thoracic pressure for neonatal respiratory distress.

26. **Medical Students in Hospitals. Department of Health 1991 HC 91(18).**
Obtaining explicit consent to participation of medical students in treatment recommended by DoH as 'best practice'.

# ▶10
## Complaints, whistle-blowing and disciplinary proceedings

### NHS complaints procedure

Procedures for complaining about services provided by the NHS were rationalised, unified and simplified in 1996 when a revised system[1], based on the recommendations of the Wilson Committee, came into effect. It is intended to be

▶ responsive, cost-effective and to enhance quality

▶ accessible, impartial and simple

▶ swift, confidential and accountable.

Disciplinary proceedings are specifically excluded, although if a complaint raises matters of sufficient significance, relevant information is to be passed to management and/or professional regulatory bodies for them to consider any other necessary steps.

The recommended procedure is in two stages:

▶ Stage I – those providing the service attempt to resolve complaint swiftly by
— an immediate, often oral, first line response
— investigation and conciliation
— action by a senior administrative officer for trust or health authority.

▶ Stage II – complainant has option of asking for a further review which *may* include consideration by a panel with lay chairman and majority of independent members.

▶ Referral to the Health Service Commissioner (Ombudsman) is available to claimants dissatisfied with the results of the independent inquiry or the decision not to convene one.

Written reports must be sent to the complainant at each stage unless immediate local resolution, made orally, was wholly effective. Reasons must be given if an independent inquiry is refused.

A non-executive director or member of the relevant trust or health authority (the 'convenor') is charged with the responsibility for deciding, in consultation with the proposed lay chairman of the panel, if an independent inquiry is to be set up. The decision is to be based on

▶ whether any further action short of an inquiry can be taken to satisfy the complainant

▶ whether all practicable action has been taken already so that an inquiry would add no further value to the process.

Two independent clinical assessors are appointed to the panel if the complaint arises from clinical decisions. Coincident with the introduction of the new complaints procedure, the powers of the Health Ombudsman were extended to include consideration of clinical decision-making.

## The complaints system in practice

Complainants, practitioners and health service managers have all expressed dissatisfaction with the new procedure. Stringent time limits have been difficult to meet and have focussed attention on the procedure rather than the principle, and the general perception of independent inquiries is that they are neither thorough nor equitable. Patients are confused by the separate routes for handling complaints and claims. Some professional staff consider that clinical complaints should be handled separately from non-clinical matters, and that there should be a seamless interface between complaints and claims, with power to award limited compensation to some complainants. The Sixth report of the the House of Commons Select Committee on Health[2], endorsed the dissatisfaction of users, advocated greater involvement of the NHS Executive, and proposed

▶ clarification and simplification of routes of access which should be widely publicised

▶ more thorough initial investigation

▶ system to be more uniform, open and transparent, and seen to be fair and independent

▶ role of convenor to be abolished

▶ complainants to have right to approach panel directly to request independent review

▶ review panels to be independent of trust or health authority subject to complaint

▶ review panels to consist of a majority of lay members, to be conducted more formally, with all parties present, and with power to summon witnesses and take evidence

▶ report of clinical assessors to be available to panel and complainant before the hearing.

The Committee's final recommendation was that the Secretary of State should consult with the Health Service Commissioner with a view to empowering him to recommend the award of an *ex gratia* payment in appropriate circumstances. Some Trusts already adopt this approach and accept an implicit merger between the handling of complaints and at least low-value claims.

## Whistle-blowing

In its revised Code of Conduct[3], the GMC reminds practitioners of a duty to protect the interests of patients if concerned about the health, conduct or performance of a colleague. It recommends local procedures for dealing with 'problem doctors' and suggests involvement of the Chairman, Chief Executive, Medical Director and Clinical Director (or corresponding post-holders), with input if necessary from specialist opinion in the relevant discipline. The Sixth Report of the Parliamentary Select Committee on Health[2] recommends that Government should take action to ensure that those who comply with this professional duty are not victimised. Statutory regulations are now in force in that the Public Interest Disclosure Act 1998 amends the terms of the Employment Rights Act 1996 to

▶ render invalid contractual terms of employment which seek to prohibit disclosure by employees of information in the public interest, and

▶ to provide remedies for employees treated detrimentally for making such disclosures.

The type of disclosure protected – information 'in the public interest' – is defined in the statute and requires genuine concern about past, current or likely malpractice, including criminal offences and attempts to conceal wrong-doing of any type which should be disclosed. Such disclosures can be made to the employer, a regulatory body or the media without loss of protection.

## Disciplinary proceedings

The *General Medical Council* is a statutory body which regulates the qualification and registration of medical practitioners under the terms of the

Medical Act 1983. Similar provisions exist for dental practitioners, nursing staff and other health care professionals. Responsibility for specialist medical training and standards rests with the Royal Colleges. Specialist accreditation is the responsibility of the Specialist Training Authority (STA) which was created by Statutory Instrument in 1995 to facilitate the free movement of doctors within the European Community.

Five committees of the GMC control fitness to practise, two of which were added to implement the Medical (Professional Performance) Act of 1995. They are

▶ Preliminary Proceedings

▶ Professional Conduct

▶ Health Committee

▶ Assessment Referral

▶ Professional Performance.

Matters which may constitute 'serious professional misconduct' are considered by the Professional Conduct Committee (PCC) after screening by the Preliminary Proceedings Committee. The Professional Conduct Committee has the power to suspend or terminate professional registration. Appeal from a punitive decision by the PCC is to the Privy Council[4,5]. In the wake of the conviction of a GP for multiple murders, both the Government and the GMC have advocated that the disciplinary procedures should be reformed and expedited. Immediate, interim suspension by the GMC during criminal investigations has been proposed and there is also pressure to limit the opportunities for practitioners suspended or removed from the register to apply for reinstatement[6]. Legislation will be needed to effect such changes to the GMC's powers.

The Health Committee of the GMC considers fitness to practice if there is evidence of physical or mental ill-health. Its conclusions can be deferred pending the outcome of treatment.

The Medical (Professional Performance) Act 1995 came into effect on July 1 1997 and only performance after that date can be subject to scrutiny. Preliminary assessment covers

▶ attitude

▶ knowledge

▶ clinical and communication skills

▶ clinical records and audit results.

Assessment is carried out by two clinicians from the relevant discipline and a lay member. Depending on the outcome, the practitioner may be required to take action to improve performance, or the case may be referred to the Professional Performance Committee with a view to imposing preconditions or suspending the practitioner's registration. The GMC recommends that referral for assessment of professional competence should only be used if attempts at local resolution are wholly inappropriate or have failed[7].

Despite attempts to modernise its procedures and image, the GMC is widely perceived as reactionary, and self-serving of the interests of doctors rather than patients. The Parliamentary Select Committee on Health[2] recommended amending the constitution of both the GMC and the corresponding regulatory body for nursing (United Kingdom Central Council of Nursing, Midwifery and Health Visiting, UKCC) to increase lay membership to a bare majority. This would effectively extinguish self-regulation, one of the fundamental elements of professionalism[8].

## Action by employing authorities

Employing authorities have a right to suspend or dismiss an employee on grounds such as gross misconduct, incompetence, or incapacity (ill-health), and can refer matters of professional competence or conduct to the General Medical Council.

A number of Health Service Circulars[9] advise on the procedures to be adopted in hospitals. Upon receipt of a written complaint and if internal review suggests there is a case to answer arising from professional (as distinct from personal) misconduct, a request is made for investigation by external assessors nominated by the Joint Consultants Committee. They report to the Medical Director who then determines what steps to take and, for serious allegations, sets up a full inquiry. The practitioner is often suspended, with full remuneration, until the inquiry has been completed. Suspension is intended as a precaution against possible harm to patients, not as a disciplinary measure, although the perception by most practitioners is of irreversible damage to reputation. .

The panel of inquiry has a legally qualified chairman and both medical and lay representatives. It meets in private and the practitioner concerned can be represented and can cross-examine witnesses. The panel reports to the employing authority which then decides whether the practitioner's employment is to be terminated. Appeals lie to the Secretary of State[10]. Provisions for the suspension of hospital practitioners are the subject of proposed new legislation[11]. A consultation document from the Chief

Medical Officer[12] also advocates radical change, with proposals for regular appraisal of all practitioners and a series of assessment centres to which those suspected of poor performance can be referred for recommendations, including retraining. Mandatory *revalidation* for all practitioners, albeit not by examination, has been accepted by the GMC and Royal Colleges and is expected to be put into effect in 2001.

General practitioners hold a contract with the local authority for the provision of services. Complaints by patients before April 1996 initiated an exploration of whether the practitioner was in breach of the terms of that contract and could culminate in the imposition of a financial penalty. This route to discipline has been terminated by the new complaints procedure. Disciplinary proceedings against general practitioners are now initiated by the Health Authority which refers the matter to the disciplinary committee of another health authority. A surviving link with the complaints procedure is that disciplinary referral can follow the report of an independent review.

Public perception of an ill-regulated profession has spawned a plethora of consultation documents and recommendations. Legal change is inevitable but primary legislation is required to amend the regulatory system. A proposal to allow government to introduce change merely by order in council was rejected before the Health Bill was enacted as the Health Act 1999.

## References

1. Acting on Complaints. Department of Health 1995.
   Government's proposals for revision to complaints handling, circulated to health authorities as EL (95) 37, responding to *Being Heard, DOH 1994*: report of Wilson Committee on NHS complaints procedures.
2. Sixth Report of the House of Commons Select Committee on Health: procedures related to adverse clinical incidents and outcomes in medical care. HMSO 1999.
   Also available at www.parliament.the-stationery-office.co.uk
3. Good Medical Practice paras 23-24. General Medical Council, July 1998.
   Duty to protect patients – what practitioners should do if concerned about a colleague.
4. Roylance v General Medical Council (on appeal to the Privy Council from the Professional Conduct Committee) [1999] Lloyd's Rep Med 139.
   Unsuccessful appeal by medically qualified Chief Executive of Bristol Royal Infirmary against finding of serious professional misconduct while engaged in administrative duties, and subsequent erasure from the medical register.
5. Stefan v General Medical Council [1999] Lloyd's Rep Med 90.
   Application to be given reasons for continued suspension. Privy Council considered there was a common law, but not statutory, duty to give sufficient information to advise practitioner in broad terms the reasons for the decision.
6. Modernising Medical Regulation: interim strengthening of GMC's fitness to practice procedure. BMJ 2000 320:890.
   Government advocates interim suspension by GMC during criminal investigation; reinstatement after being struck off should only be in exceptional circumstances. For expediting disciplinary proceedings see *BMJ 2000 320:466*.

7. Maintaining Good Medical Practice. General Medical Council, July 1998.
   See also specific guidance from GMC in *Performance Procedures: a guide to the new arrangements. July 1998.*

8. Irvine D. The performance of doctors: the new professionalism. Lancet 1999 353:1174.
   GMC President reminds practitioners: professional independence is a privilege requiring competent self-regulation.

9. Health Circular (90) 9. Department of Health, 1990.
   Recommendations for conduct of disciplinary hearings into conduct or competence of hospital practitioners. Updates HC (82) 13 which advised setting up of 'Three Wise Men' procedure to consider physical or mental incapacity.

10. Annexure C of Health Circular (90) 9.
    Sets out the procedure for appeal against dismissal which was originally contained in paragraph 190 of the Hospital Medical and Dental Whitley Council Agreement (Whitley Council 'Terms and Conditions of Service').

11. Suspension of Hospital Medical Practitioners Bill, February 2000.
    Proposals from House of Lords, available at www.publications.parliament.uk
    Recommends there should be no suspension unless specific procedure, set out in the Bill, has been followed. Decision is to be taken expeditiously by Chief Executive. Bill includes provisions for appeal.

12. Supporting doctors, protecting patients: consultation paper on preventing, recognising, and dealing with poor clinical performance of doctors in England. Department of Health 1999.
    Chief Medical Officer's proposals for regular reappraisal and new system for identifying and assisting poor performers.

# ▶11

# Doctors and the coroner's court

Proceedings in the coroner's court are governed by statute (The Coroners Act 1988), supplemented by The Coroners Rules 1984. Coroners are appointed by a county council, metropolitan or borough council and are identified by the district for which they are responsible. The majority are solicitors but some are medically or dually qualified; a minimum of five years experience is required in either case. Only a minority are full-time coroners.

Apart from an historical role to investigate the finding of treasure trove, the duty of the coroner is restricted to the investigation of certain deaths. He is charged with a duty to make enquiry

▶ when informed that the body of a person is lying within his jurisdiction *and*

▶ there is reasonable cause to suspect that the death was

▶ either violent or unnatural

▶ or sudden and of unknown cause

▶ or occurred in prison

▶ or in such place or circumstances as to require an inquest pursuant to any other Act.

It is not necessary for the death itself to have occurred within the jurisdiction.

A jury *can* be called for any inquest but *must* be called if the death occurred

▶ in prison

▶ while the deceased was in police custody or resulted from injury caused by a police officer in the execution of his duty

▶ as a consequence of accident, poisoning or disease, notice of which is required to be given under any Act eg Health and Safety at Work Act 1974

▶ in circumstances the continuance or possible recurrence of which is prejudicial to the health or safety of the public or any section thereof.

The jury at an inquest is composed of not less than seven and not more than eleven jurors.

## Duty to inform the coroner

Medical practitioners commonly sign a 'death certificate' but this does no more than certify the cause of death. Note that when criteria for brain stem death have been fulfilled, the time of death is deemed to be no later than when the first set of tests was completed[1]. The legal death certificate is issued by the Registrar of Births and Deaths. There is no *obligation* on the medical practitioner to report deaths which could lie within the criteria enumerated above, but it is courteous and sensitive to do so. The Registrar will report the death to the coroner if he is not prepared to issue a formal death certificate on the information received.

Death should be reported to the coroner in the following circumstances:

- the cause is unknown

- the practitioner has not attended the deceased during his last illness

- the practitioner *neither* attended the deceased during the last 14 days before death *nor* saw the body after death

- death occurred during an operation or before recovery from the effects of an anaesthetic

- death was caused by industrial disease or poisoning

- any death believed to unnatural or caused by violence, neglect or abortion.

Some of these terms are imprecise, particularly 'unnatural' when applied to the elderly and infirm. However, a coroner informed of such a death has a *discretion* to dispense with an inquest, with or without a post mortem examination, and can then notify the Registrar of his decision.

## The coroner's post mortem examination

The coroner has jurisdiction over the body once a death has been reported to him. He can order a post mortem examination to be undertaken by a practitioner of his choice. When death occurs in the course of medical treatment, particularly if anxieties have been expressed about the standard of care, the post mortem is usually carried out at another location by an independent pathologist. The pathologist's report is addressed to the coroner and is confidential unless he authorises disclosure. Post mortem material *of potential relevance to the cause of death* can be retained at the discretion of the pathologist but only for such period as the coroner thinks fit.

## The inquest

An inquest is an inquiry, not a trial. However, grievances as well as grief are often manifest and, particularly if there are legal representatives, the questioning can be quite hostile. It is up to the coroner to restrict questions to the matters to be explored, namely

► who the deceased was

► when, where and how the deceased came by his death.

The question 'how' is interpreted restrictively to mean 'by what means' rather than 'in what broad circumstances'[2] but the coroner is still expected to make full, fair and fearless enquiry[3]. Resolution of these apparently conflicting requirements is a matter for the coroner's discretion.

Most inquests are opened and adjourned soon after the death and only evidence of identity is submitted. This suffices for the coroner to provide relatives with a certificate for burial, cremation or removal of the body outside England. Disposal is not authorised if criminal charges are likely.

The inquest is resumed after relevant witness statements have been obtained. The proceedings are formal but less so than in other courts. The coroner examines on oath or affirmation those witnesses who, in his opinion, can contribute evidence relevant to the questions listed above. The witnesses can then be cross-examined by 'properly interested persons' or their representatives, for example the family of the deceased, or the police if the death occurred in custody. Medical practitioners may be called upon to give evidence concerning

► the post mortem examination

► the deceased's health and habits during life (eg smoking, drug or alcohol addiction)

► medical aspects of the deceased's terminal illness.

No witness is obliged to answer any question tending to incriminate him, and the coroner is prohibited from framing a verdict in such a way as to appear to determine any question of civil liability, or of criminal liability on the part of a named person. If, during the course of an inquest, it appears to the coroner that a person may be charged with a specific offence such as murder or manslaughter, he must adjourn the hearing and report to the Director of Public Prosecutions. This procedure is followed if the coroner considers there could be a finding of criminal negligence.

Inquests into deaths occurring in the course of, or as a result of, medical treatment are the source of most concern to practitioners. They or their hospital are likely to be represented by a medical defence organisation or hospital solicitor, particularly if grievances are suspected or the family is to be legally represented (despite the non-availability of legal aid for representation at inquests). Disclosure of hospital notes, records and internal inquiry reports is covered in chapter 8. A witness who fails to attend when summoned may be found guilty of contempt of court[4] and reluctant witnesses may be served with a subpoena. It is also an offence to refuse to answer questions, withhold information, or give evidence known to be erroneous while on oath.

## The coroner's verdict

The verdict is the totality of the findings made by the coroner or the jury but the term is often used merely to refer to the conclusion. Certain terms are recommended, the most common being

▶ death from natural causes

▶ industrial disease

▶ dependent or non-dependent abuse of drugs

▶ accident or misadventure

▶ suicide

▶ unlawful killing

▶ open verdict.

Note that a finding of still-birth negates the rest of the inquiry – the infant has not had life independent from its mother. Suicide and unlawful killing both require proof beyond reasonable doubt whereas all other verdicts can be made on the balance of probabilities. An open verdict is reserved for cases where there is insufficient evidence to reach any of the other conclusions.

## Accident or misadventure in the context of deaths related to medical treatment

There is judicial authority for the view that the term 'misadventure' is obsolete[5] but many coroners continue to use it. Defined as the unintended adverse outcome of an intentional, lawful act, it is well suited to many deaths occurring in the course of treatment. It does *not* carry any implication of negligence, nor does it refute the possibility of such a finding in a civil court[6]. Many families find the term more acceptable than mere 'accident', with its connotation that the cause of death was independent of any human intervention when it manifestly was not.

## A descriptive verdict

When death occurs in the course of a potentially fatal condition and medical intervention fails to prevent the death, a conclusion of 'natural causes' is correct. If the circumstances surrounding the death are exceptional, the verdict can incorporate a brief, neutral factual statement[7].

## 'Lack of care' as a rider to the verdict

This is a phrase where the strict legal definition of 'care' is of paramount importance. It refers to care in the narrow, physical sense and has ***nothing to do with negligence or breach of duty***[3].

The concept is of 'neglect' – gross failure to provide food, liquid, shelter, warmth or basic medical attention for someone in a dependent position who cannot provide it for himself. Neglect (or self-neglect) should not form part of the verdict unless a clear and direct causal connection with the death can be established. Despite these defining criteria, attempts are still made by legal representatives appearing for families of patients dying in contentious circumstances to persuade the coroner to find 'lack of care'. Such applications rarely succeed but may herald a civil claim, or reflect a wish for public obloquy when civil action is impractical, usually for financial reasons. A finding of lack of care requires evidence of *absence* of care, not possibly erroneous care[8-10].

## Recommendations by the coroner

The coroner, but not a coroner's jury, has power to refer matters to the appropriate authority if by so doing it would enable changes to be made to prevent repetition of similar fatalities.

# Challenge to decisions of the coroner

Application to challenge the decision of a coroner, including a decision not to hold an inquest[11], is made either by seeking leave for judicial review or by the statutory power of obtaining the *fiat* of the Attorney-General. The appeal is heard by the Divisional Court, a subdivision of the High Court usually constituted by a Lord Justice of Appeal and a High Court Judge. There is potential for appeal from the Divisonal Court to the Court of Appeal. In general the courts are reluctant to order a new inquest unless it is likely that a different conclusion would be reached[12].

## References

1. Re A [1992] 3 Med LR 303.
   Brain stem death after alleged non-accidental injury in child of 19 months. Court has jurisdiction to declare patient dead for all legal as well as medical purposes, from date of completion of first set of tests for brain stem death.
2. R v HM Coroner for Western District of East Sussex *ex parte* Homberg, Roberts and Manners (1994) 158 JP 357.
   Challenge to conduct of an inquest into deaths caused by arson. The inquiry must focus on matters directly causative of death. 'How' means by what means, not in what broad circumstances.
3. R v HM Coroner for N Humberside *ex parte* Jamieson [1994] 3 WLR 82.
   Court of Appeal hearing arising from suicide of a prisoner. Extensive review of history and function of coroner's court is followed by a summary of current role and, most importantly, definitive criteria for a finding of 'lack of care'.
4. Re Dr AS Ryan (1984) 148 JP 569.
   Police surgeon summoned to give evidence at an inquest failed to arrive in time and was ordered to pay a fine. Decision challenged successfully – he had not been properly summoned and could give good explanation for delay.
5. R v HM Coroner for Portsmouth *ex parte* Anderson [1987] 1 WLR 1640.
   Death of a serviceman from hyperpyrexia; finding of 'accidental death' challenged unsuccessfully. The distinction between 'accident' and 'misadventure' was deemed to be without purpose or effect. Note however the acceptance in *R v Southwark Coroner ex parte Fields 1998 162 JP 411* of misadventure as a sub-heading of accidental death.
6. R v HMCoroner for Birmingham & Solihull *ex parte* Cotton (1996) 160 JP 123.
   Challenge to verdict of natural causes: hospital death from pneumonia in sedated patient with alcoholic liver disease, gastro-intestinal bleeding and smoking-related lung damage. Purpose of an inquest is to discover the cause of death, not get a negligence claim on its feet. Questions of medical negligence should be tried by a Judge on a pleaded case.
7. R v HM Coroner for Birmingham & Solihull *ex parte* Benton [1997] 8 Med LR 362.
   2-year old with laryngo-tracheo-bronchitis died from bilateral tension pneumothoraces and surgical emphysema soon after emergency bronchoscopy undertaken after prolonged delay in securing hospital admission. Jury permitted only to consider verdict of death from natural causes which they endorsed by majority of 8:1. Challenge to verdict upheld only in so far as possibility of accident/misadventure should have been left for jury to consider. Finding of 'natural causes' was quashed and a descriptive account was to be given for cause of death. New inquest not ordered.
8. R v HM Coroner for Surrey *ex parte* Wright [1997] 1 All ER 823
   Fit Afro-Carribean 27-years old died from cerebral damage after anoxic incident during GA for dental extraction. Verdict of accidental death challenged on several grounds including "If this is not a case of lack of care, what is?" Verdict upheld; no new inquest ordered. Re-emphasis on 'matters of negligence are better decided in a civil action'.

9. **R v HM Coroner for Wiltshire** *ex parte* **Clegg (1997) 161 JP 521.**

   Deceased took an overdose of aspirin and died about 12 hours after admission to hospital. Coroner did not receive, or call for, any medical evidence relating to hospital admission, a fact known to hospital staff. Verdict of suicide. Two years later, independent review set up in response to parental complaints, was highly critical of all aspects of management. New inquest then sought. Court expressed concern at lack of obligation to volunteer information, considered finding of neglect contributing to the death *might* have been made, but this did not warrant new inquest.

10. **R v HM Coroner for Coventry** *ex parte* **O'Reilly (1996) 160 JP 749.**

    Deceased had fallen at home and, believed to be drunk, was taken into custody. Transferred to hospital 13 hours later, deeply unconscious, where CT showed large intra-cerebral haematoma. Challenge to verdict of accidental death upheld and new inquest ordered. No reason in principle or logic why accidental death aggravated by lack of care should not be appropriate if circumstances justify, despite obstacle of proving a causal link.

11. **R v HM Coroner for Avon** *ex parte* **Smith (1998) 162 JP 403.**

    Coroner declined to hold an inquest into death of 14 year-old in hospital, admitted with cerebral symptoms. CT, which showed cerebellar haemorrhage, not performed for 10 hours despite concern of parents who had earlier lost a son from a 'cerebral episode'. Internal and external enquiries exonerated hospital staff; coroner stated no grounds for inquest because death was 'not unnatural'. Inquest ordered – question of 'natural causes' warranted investigation.

12. **R v HM Coroner for Derbyshire (Scarsdale)** *ex parte* **Fletcher (1992) 156 JP 522.**

    Deceased had worked as a miner from age 14 – 50 years. Died aged 65 from chronic obstructive pulmonary disease and congestive cardiomyopathy. Reported to pneumoconiosis medical panel who concluded pneumoconiosis neither caused nor materially accelerated death. Verdict of natural causes. During investigation to secure compensation, new expert report suggested pneumoconiosis *was* a contributory factor. Unusually, a new inquest was ordered. Normally mere differences of opinion between experts do not suffice: new *evidence* not new *interpretation* is needed.

# ▶12

# Doctors and the criminal law

The essential difference between a civil and a criminal offence is that one reflects conflict between two or more individuals and is aimed at securing recompense, whereas the other is conflict between an individual and society with a view to punishment. Minor criminal offences are dealt with in the **Magistrates Court** but matters of greater importance are heard in the **Crown Court** by a Judge sitting with a jury whose members are the representatives of society. Doctors are not immune from criminality but prosecutions brought against individual practitioners are considered here only in the context of criminal charges arising from deaths associated with clinical practice.

Conviction for a criminal offence requires proof beyond reasonable doubt that

▶ the person charged has carried out an unlawful act (*'actus reus'*) and

▶ in doing so had the necessary guilty state of mind (*'mens rea'*).

Specific 'elements' for each offence define the unlawful act and the necessary guilty state of mind. Both must be made out if the prosecution is to succeed (cf the civil claimant's need to establish both breach of duty and causation), but a finding of guilt can still be diminished or even avoided if the defendant can advance a valid defence (for example, provocation in the context of murder).

The standard of proof required in a criminal case – beyond reasonable doubt – is higher than the balance of probabilities which suffices for civil actions. Another practical distinction is that the legal rules of evidence are observed more stringently in criminal matters. The phrase 'beyond reasonable doubt' does not mean 'beyond a shadow of doubt'. A remote possibility, which is not in the least probable, does not create 'reasonable doubt'. The Judge directs the jury on the standard required, often telling them 'they must be satisfied so that they are sure'.

# Homicide

Homicide is the unlawful killing of a human being, identified in the context of infants as a life independent from the mother. Murder and manslaughter are both homicide, distinguished by the the state of mind of the defendant and the perceived culpability so determined.

   *The cause of death* must be attributable to the unlawful act, as a matter of fact and of law. Causation in fact is determined by the 'but for' test – but for the act in question, would the victim have died? Causation in law requires exploration of the closeness of the link between the act and the death. Was the act a substantial and operating factor? An example helps to explain this concept – a victim is knocked unconscious and left on the shore where he drowns when the tide comes in. The factual cause of death is drowning: the cause in law is the act of the defendant. Undue vulnerability of the victim (the 'eggshell skull' rule) does not exonerate the perpetrator.

   The importance of the distinction between causation in fact and in law is apparent when considering the role of medical interventions. Thus two assailants, each convicted of murder, appealed on the grounds that a subsequent medical decision to withdraw mechanical ventilation caused the deaths[1]. Both appeals failed. Even clinical negligence as an intervening event will not *necessarily* displace responsibility for an unlawful death (eg murder)[2]. Similarly, when considering an application for a declaration that withdrawal of mechanical ventilation from a patient with exceptionally severe Guillain-Barre syndrome would not be unlawful[3], a New Zealand court accepted that the cause of death would be the disease and not the act of withdrawal, *provided* the decision to withdraw ventilation had been made in accordance with good medical practice. Thus the *propriety* of the medical act which intervenes between initiating event or illness and the fatal outcome is to be taken into consideration when considering the legal cause of death, as well as the *magnitude* of the contribution of each element to the death.

   *Intention to kill* or to cause serious injury is a prerequisite for a conviction of murder. Primary or specific purpose intent exists when a person sets out to secure an objective by whatever means lie within his power. Secondary intent (also known as indirect or foresight intent) is a presumption: a man is presumed to intend the consequences of his act if the outcome is a virtual certainty and he is aware, when acting, that this is so. Evidence must be adduced in each case to satisfy the jury to the requisite standard that these conditions were, in fact, fulfilled. An important distinction must be drawn between intention and motive. Intention refers to what the actor seeks to achieve; motive is the reason for acting. A benevolent motive does not displace a criminal conviction for murder if the intention to kill is made out at trial[4].

*Voluntary manslaughter* is the likely verdict if a defendant is found guilty of causing death and of having the intention to kill but has successfully pleaded one of a number of defences, usually provocation or diminished responsibility. The significance lies in the sentence. Murder carries a mandatory life sentence whereas sentencing for manslaughter is at the discretion of the judge.

*Involuntary manslaughter* is a verdict which follows a finding that the defendant caused the death, but without any intention to kill or cause serious injury. It includes death occurring as the result of an unlawful act or, most common in the context of medical manslaughter, as a consequence of what has variously been described as 'recklessness' or 'gross negligence'. The discussion here is restricted to gross negligence in the discharge of professional responsibilities.

## Manslaughter by gross negligence

It is arguable that deaths arising as a result of medical treatment can be distinguished from the usual case of homicide because it is the defendant's professional obligations which require him to deal with a pre-existing danger which is not of his own making. This philosophy lay behind the original definition of gross (ie criminal) negligence[5] which required

- the existence of a duty of care
- breach of the duty
- death occurring as a consequence of the breach of duty
- negligence which went beyond a mere matter of compensation between the parties.

The first three elements of this test are identical to those set out in chapter 2 as the basis for a *civil* claim in negligence. The fourth is the dimension which adds criminality – showing such disregard for the safety of others amounted to a crime against the State and was deserving of punishment.

After some years when 'gross negligence' was regarded by the courts as synonymous with recklessness, the importance of specific criteria for a finding of gross negligence in the discharge of professional responsibilities was re-emphasised by the Court of Appeal in the course of three appeals, heard simultaneously, against convictions for manslaughter by an electrician, two junior doctors, and a locum anaesthetist[6]. Two of the appeals succeeded but the third did not. The third appellant appealed, unsuccessfully, to the House of Lords[7] when the criteria for a finding of involuntary manslaughter by breach of duty suggested by the Court of Appeal were confirmed as

▶ the existence of a duty

▶ breach of the duty causing death

▶ gross negligence which the jury considered justified a criminal conviction.

The third of these is the only one which differs in terminology, if not in meaning, from the original definition of 'gross negligence'. A jury is entitled to make a finding of gross negligence if evidence is adduced to show that the defendant

▶ was indifferent to an obvious risk of injury to health

▶ had actual foresight of the risk but determined nevertheless to run it

▶ appreciated the risk and intended to avoid it but displayed such a high degree of negligence in the attempted avoidance as the jury considered justified conviction

▶ displayed inattention or failure to advert to a serious risk which went beyond 'mere inadvertence' in respect of an obvious and important matter which the defendant's duty demanded he should address.

Given these directions, it is the *jury* which decides whether the evidence suffices to fulfil one or more of the criteria and, if so, whether the charge of gross negligence has been made out.

## Criminal liability for end-of-life decisions

The conviction of a caring doctor for attempted murder[4], followed shortly by a House of Lords decision that it would not be unlawful to withdraw artificial nutrition and hydration from a patient in persistent vegetative state[8], led to the setting up of a House of Lords Committee[9] to consider the ethical, legal and clinical implications of end-of life decision-making. The recommendations of the Committee were conservative:

▶ the law should not be changed to permit active euthanasia

▶ the right of competent patients to refuse medical treatment was strongly endorsed

- the law on suicide[10] should not be changed

- there should be no new offence of 'mercy-killing'

- the mandatory life-sentence for murder should be dropped.

All but the last of the recommendations were accepted by government. The Committee also acknowledged that it is lawful – indeed proper – to administer drugs to relieve pain notwithstanding an awareness of the probability that they will hasten death, a view confirmed in caselaw both before and after the report was published[11,12]. The essential legal element is the intention of the practitioner – if the primary intention is to relieve suffering, the *mens rea* for a finding of murder is absent. The practitioner may foresee that death is virtually certain after, and perhaps as a consequence of the treatment, but the presumption that he therefore intends the death is refuted by evidence that his primary intent is to benefit the patient. Some regard this argument as specious – and perhaps in practice it is.

*Termination of life-support* is followed by death in stark, temporal proximity. The practitioner is protected from a charge of murder if the decision accords with good medical practice. There is no obligation to continue treatment deemed to be futile or not in the patient's best interests, but evidence must be available to support this contention[13]. Particular difficulty is associated with the chronic stable condition of persistent vegetative state. The House of Lords has accepted that 'treatment' can include nutrition and hydration when provided by artificial means[8]. In that case, the severity of the neurological damage was deemed such that either the patient had no best interests or they were not served by continued treatment. However, the decision was not to be used as a precedent – parliament, not the courts, should be responsible for formulating principle. Thus a declaration by the court should be obtained if the withdrawal of nutrition and hydration is contemplated from a profoundly damaged but physiologically stable patient[14]. Perceived conflict over the status of nutrition and hydration as 'treatment' or 'basic humanitarian care' means that particular care is necessary before taking such a step in any circumstances[15]. The present position is unsatisfactory because the limits of legality are not clearly defined. A private member's bill – Medical Treatment (Prevention of Euthanasia) – which sought to prohibit the withholding or withdrawing of medical treatment, including hydration and nutrition, when this would bring about the death of the patient, was rejected.

*Withholding treatment* is acceptable practice *provided* the treating practitioner genuinely and for good reason believes it to be in the best interests of the patient to do so[16]. The court will not dictate what is appropriate treatment[17]. The apparent discrepancy between the court's power to over-rule parental decisions to withhold consent and its reluctance to order treatment requested by parents but resisted by the practitioner, reflects the principle that what is done should be in the best interests of the patient and that is primarily a matter of expert opinion.

## The law as a vehicle for social change

In 1939 an eminent gynaecologist announced that he intended to terminate the pregnancy of a 14-year old victim of gang rape. He duly did so at a prestigious London hospital. He was prosecuted and acquitted on a technicality of interpretation of the then-relevant statute[18]. The case focussed attention on the fact that abortion, although unlawful, was widely practised, albeit in circumstances which were often unhygienic and dangerous. Subsequent caselaw reflected this liberal statutory interpretation and was followed ultimately in 1967 by the first Abortion Act. A number of controversial social and ethical issues have since prompted responsive legislation, often without a legal test case. Some examples include The Human Organ Transplantation Act 1989, The Human Fertilisation and Embryology Act 1990 and the Surrogacy Arrangements Act 1985. The law – whether it is defined in the courts or established by legislation – sets the limits of what is deemed to be acceptable practice. It is not immutable but can and does change in response to new developments or social pressures. There is no reason why medical practitioners, parliamentarians or judges should be the sole arbiters of ethical dilemmas, but rules need to be set and the law is empowered to fulfil that role. It is the duty of all citizens – including medical practitioners – to abide by the law and, if the law assists in defining the boundaries of acceptable medical practice, its intervention is to be welcomed, not feared.

## References

1. R v Malcherek; R v Steel [1981] 2 All ER 422.
   Discontinuing mechanical ventilation did not suffice to interrupt the chain of causation between initial assault upon each of two victims and their subsequent death. Appeals against convictions for murder failed.
2. R v Cheshire [1991] 1 WLR 844
   Failure to recognise tracheal stricture the proximate cause of death of a victim who had been shot 5 weeks earlier. Defendant's appeal against conviction of murder was unsuccessful.
3. Auckland Area Health Board v Attorney-General [1993] 4 Med LR 239.
   New Zealand declaration that it would be lawful to withdraw mechanical ventilation from a patient severely affected by Guillain Barre syndrome. Questions explored were whether death was caused by the disease (yes) or the withdrawal of ventilation, and whether mechanical ventilation was a necessity of life (not in these circumstances).

4. **R v Cox (1992) 12 BMLR 38; (and see legal commentary in BMJ 1992 305:731).**
   Conviction for attempted murder (cause of death unproven because body had been cremated before charges were brought). Consultant Rheumatologist administered intravenous potassium chloride to a woman terminally ill from chronic rheumatoid arthritis, in 'uncontrollable' pain, who begged to die and whose family supported her decision.

5. **R v Bateman (1925) LJKB 791**
   Gross, fatal, pelvic visceral injury during attempted home delivery. Criteria for gross negligence defined.

6. **R v Holloway; R v Adomako; R v Prentice & Sullman [1993] 4 Med LR 304.**
   This report does not include the facts of R v Holloway – an electrician whose faulty wiring of a central heating system caused death by electrocution – but the Court of Appeal set out principles applying to all three cases. The anaesthetic death involved failure to recognise disconnection of the ventilator; the third case arose from a fatal injection of vincristine into the theca of a patient receiving regular intrathecal methotrexate and intravenous vincristine. The appeals of Holloway, Prentice and Sullman were allowed, their convictions being quashed. Adomako's appeal failed.

7. **R v Adomako [1994] 5 Med LR 277.**
   Appeal to the House of Lords by the unsuccessful appellant (an anaesthetist) from (6) above also failed. It is sufficient to direct the jury to adopt the criteria for gross negligence set out by the Court of Appeal in this case.

8. **Airedale NHS Trust v Bland [1993] 4 Med LR 39.**
   House of Lords decision that withdrawal of artificial nutrition and hydration from a patient in persistent vegetative state would not be unlawful. Their Lordships specifically stated the decision should *not* be regarded as a precedent.

9. **Select Committee on Medical Ethics, House of Lords Report. HMSO 1994.**
   Legal and ethical analysis of end of life decisions. Law should not be changed to permit active euthanasia. Offence of 'mercy-killing' not recommended; suggestion to drop mandatory life sentence for murder rejected by government.

10. **Suicide Act 1961**
    Suicide is no longer a criminal offence but section 2 preserves aiding and abetting suicide as an offence.

11. **R v Bodkin Adams [1957] Crim LR 365.**
    GP acquitted of murder by administration of increasing doses of opiates to elderly patients with a view to personal gain. See also *R v Arthur (1981) 12 BMLR 1*; acquittal of consultant paediatrician charged with attempted murder by prescribing 'dihydrocodeine and nursing care only' for a neonate with Down's syndrome, rejected by her mother.

12. **Dyer C. BMJ 1999 318:1306.**
    Unwise public declaration by a GP that he had helped a number of patients to have pain-free deaths led to prosecution for murder. Unanimous verdict of 'not guilty'. GP's considerate treatment was applauded by the judge. See *Gillon R, Doyal L BMJ 1999 318:1431* for discussion of ethical doctrine of 'double effect'.

13. **South Buckinghamshire NHS Trust v R (A Patient) [1996] 7 Med LR 401.**
    23-year old existed in a 'low awareness state'. No obligation to treat if, in all the circumstances, life would be so afflicted as to be intolerable. See also (8) above where treatment withdrawal was justified on grounds of futility.

14. **Wade DT, Johnston C. The permanent vegetative state. BMJ 1999 319:841.**
    Review of clinical features plus practical guide on steps required to obtain court's approval to discontinue treatment.

15. **Bliss MR. BMJ 2000 320:67**
    Critical analysis by a consultant geriatrician of the reprimand and suspension of a GP for ordering withdrawal of nutritional supplements from a demented elderly patient. Reported to police by nurses; police referred to GMC.

16. **Re J (A Minor) [1993] 4 Med LR 21.**
    Infant with profound neurological disability and frequent convulsions compromising respiration. Court of Appeal reversed a decision requiring that child be given life-prolonging treatment, including mechanical ventilation. There was no obligation to provide treatment which, in *bona fide* opinion of practitioner, is not in patient's best interests. 'Wholly inconsistent with the law' to order treatment contrary to doctor's clinical judgment.

17. R v Portsmouth Hospital NHS Trust [1999] Lloyd's Rep Med 367.

Seriously disabled 12-year old given morphine against wishes of mother and a non-consensual DNR order was written. Violence followed between staff and family. Application for Judicial Review of the Trust's decision failed. Court of Appeal held it was inappropriate for court to declare what a hospital should or should not do as a matter of law. Individual cases of conflict should be resolved at the time by referral to Family Division of the High Court for declaration of child's best interests, or application under s8 Children's Act 1989, or make child a ward of court.

18. R v Bourne [1939] 1 KB 687.

Criminal prosecution for procuring a miscarriage. Not unlawful if done in good faith for sole purpose of preserving the life of the mother – interpreted to include adverse consequences to physical health short of death.

# ▶ Glossary of legal terms and phrases

| | |
|---|---|
| **Act of parliament**: | completed parliamentary legislation |
| ***Actus reus***: | factual element of a criminal offence |
| **ADR**: | alternative Dispute Resolution – alternatives to litigation |
| **Aggravated damages**: | additional compensation for injurious personal conduct |
| **Appellate Courts**: | courts hearing appeals from decisions of a lower court or judicial officer |
| **Assault**: | threat causing apprehension of immediate physical contact |
| **Battery**: | non-consensual touching |
| **Burden of proof**: | party on whom onus lies to prove its case |
| **CFA**: | conditional Fee Agreement |
| **Civil law**: | civil legal procedure derived from Roman law |
| **CNST**: | clinical Negligence Scheme for Trusts |
| **Common law**: | body of decided English legal cases, ie 'caselaw' |
| **Competence**: | sufficiency of mental faculties to take legally valid decisions |
| **Consideration**: | the price of a contractual agreement |
| **Contract**: | a legally enforceable agreement |
| **Damages**: | financial compensation |
| **Inquest and inquisition**: | proceedings and conclusion of coroner's court |
| **Issue of proceedings**: | first formal step in civil litigation |
| **Judicial Review**: | remedy for wrongful exercise of administrative power |
| **Legal aid**: | state funded financial assistance for legal proceedings |
| **Limitation**: | extinguishing of legal right of action by passage of time |
| **Litigation Friend**: | court-approved legal representative |
| ***Mens rea***: | a criminally culpable state of mind |
| **Misadventure**: | a sub-section of accident |
| **Misfeasance**: | wrong-doing |
| **Multiplicand**: | net annual value of an on-going loss |

| | |
|---|---|
| **Multiplier**: | variable reflecting period of a loss, discounted for early receipt |
| **Neglect**: | gross failure to provide basic necessities |
| **Negligence**: | culpable transgression of a duty |
| **NHSLA**: | national Health Service Litigation Authority |
| **Parliamentary Bill**: | a proposed item of parliamentary legislation |
| **Particulars of Claim**: | formal statement of claimant's case |
| **Pleadings**: | collection of formal documents encapsulating an action |
| | the term Statement of Case is now preferred |
| **Precedent**: | a binding judicial decision |
| **Privy Council**: | body of advisers to the Sovereign, appointed on the advice of Ministers |
| | Judicial Committee of Privy Council hears appeals, eg from professional disciplinary bodies |
| **Proceedings**: | formal legal action |
| **Quantum**: | the financial value of a claim for compensation |
| ***Res ipsa loquitur***: | aphorism meaning 'the thing speaks for itself' |
| **Service (of documents)**: | delivery by a legally accepted method |
| **Standard of proof**: | degree of certainty to be achieved for an action to succeed |
| **Statement of case**: | term introduced by Civil Procedure Rules 1999 to replace Pleadings |
| **Statute**: | an Act of Parliament |
| **Statutory Instrument**: | subordinate (delegated) legislation permitted by a parent Act |
| **Tort**: | civil wrong-doing not including breach of contract |
| **Vicarious liability**: | liability for injury caused by another – eg an employee |

# ▶ Index